The
Southern Way

The regular volume for the Southern devotee

Kevin Robertson

Issue 38

www.crecy.co.uk

© 2017 Crécy Publishing Ltd
and the various contributors

ISBN 9781909328624

First published in 2017 by Noodle Books
an imprint of Crécy Publishing Ltd

All editorial submissions to:
The Southern Way (Kevin Robertson)
Conway
Warnford Rd
Corhampton
Hants SO32 3ND
Tel: 01489 877880
editorial@thesouthernway.co.uk

Publisher's note: Every effort has been made to
identify and correctly attribute photographic
credits. Any error that may have occurred is
entirely unintentional.
In line with the new design the front cover image has
changed from that originally advertised. All other
information is unaffected.

Printed in Malta by Melita Press

Noodle Books is an imprint of
Crécy Publishing Limited
1a Ringway Trading Estate
Shadowmoss Road
Manchester M22 5LH

www.crecy.co.uk

Issue No 39 of THE SOUTHERN WAY
ISBN 9781909328631
available in July 2017 at £14.95
To receive your copy the moment it is
released, order in advance from your usual
supplier, or it can be sent post-free (UK)
direct from the publisher:

Crécy Publishing Ltd

1a Ringway Trading Estate, Shadowmoss
Road, Manchester M22 5LH

Tel 0161 499 0024

www.crecy.co.uk

enquiries@crecy.co.uk

Front Cover:
In the same way that in the past photographs were
taken at Nine Elms of an earlier generation of motive
power lined in similar fashion, here we have four Class
33 diesel-electric locos posed this time outside the front
of Eastleigh diesel depot – no numbers I am afraid. At
first glance all would appear identical but I would cover
myself by stating I am sure the experts on the Class 33
type may know different. One snippet of history on
these machines that came to light recently was that the
requirement of BR for a number of narrow-bodied
examples intended for work on the Hastings line and
referred to as 'Slim-Jims' was enough to cause severe
financial difficulties to builders, the Birmingham Railway
Carriage and Wagon Company. This may well have
contributed to its demise soon after the last of the Class
33 type were delivered in 1962. Despite the design
being fifty or more years old, at the time of writing
three examples remain in use on the public network
with another twenty-nine preserved, although by no
means are all of these operational.

Rear Cover:
Having had 'modern traction' for the front we should at
least have something 'steamified' on the reverse:
represented here by No 30782 'Sir Brian' at Salisbury on
14th May 1962 with empty ballast hoppers for Meldon.
A Bournemouth based engine since 1951, this was its
last summer in service being withdrawn week ending
27th September 1962. *Alan A. Jarvis / SLS collection*

Title page:
The reality of steam engine storage/maintenance in the
1950s. Part of Bricklayers Arms depot with a line-up of
SECR 'H' class tank engines led by No 31533 and also a
Brighton E6 No 32410. Behind the latter is a pair of
Bulleid tenders. *E. R. Wethersett*

Contents

Introduction

There are advantages, but also disadvantages, to having the editor's pen (should that be keyboard?) to hand every three months – unless that is as per next time when I have persuaded our friend Chris Sayers-Leavy to take up the cudgel so to speak and pen something on his own pet topic. So, what do I write, a promise of what is to come, continuing on the theme of something that is topical in the railway press or on one of the various discussion groups, or perhaps even something totally different? Well this time it is going to be in the last category and indeed a topic that has been rumbling around in the grey matter for quite a while now, hence it is time to use the opportunity presented here.

From the outset *Southern Way* has been an historic publication. Where history starts and ends is subjective and I do regularly receive correspondence and suggestions about ideas for articles and periods to cover. It would be all too easy to fill each issue with topics that were solely of personal interest, I hope I have avoided too much of that in the past, but what I have learned is that generally we are a broadminded lot and as such I feel happy at setting off with what follows – 'the modern railway'.

As a prelude to what is to follow in SW39 due in July, we have pleasure in including another of the Jim Seddon images, this time of what was by then the oldest locomotive at work on the Southern Region at the end of steam: No 35003 seen here approaching Byfleet and New Haw on 1st July 1967 with the 0835 ex Waterloo. The steam era might be drawing to a close but the memories remain, such as years before when an unidentified 'MN' ran at 98 mph between Tonbridge and Ashford.... . As July 1067 approached there were also many reports of speed on 6.15pm from Weymouth to Waterloo, the highest speeds usually recorded between Basingstoke and Woking. No 35003 was just one example, with a trailing load of just 170 tons the engine was worked to 89 at Hook, 103 between Winchfield and Fleet and on another occasion 101.4 between same two station. Then there was sister engine No 35007: 62 at Worting, 89 at Basingstoke, 91 at Hook, 98 at Winchfield and another at 103 at Fleet, the (un-named)driver attempting to make up time but thwarted when further checks ruined his chances. Finally as late as the 8th July 1967, No 35008 left Southampton with 355 toms 16 minutes late but managed to arrive at Waterloo 7 early. Finally No 34023 with a trailing load of 300 tons was recorded as making 91 at Hersham. When asked later the laconic reply from the driver was, 'Well, he – indicating the fireman, filled the box up at Woking and I thought I might as well burn it.' Hence the reports of red hot lumps of coal being ejected from chimney and causing several lineside spectators to turn and watch as the fiery apparition sizzled past.
Jim Seddon

Fear not. I am not going to comment about how I miss this and that, history can sometimes be perceived as rose-tinted and I am determined not to go down that path. Neither am I going to take a deliberate swipe at the operators currently running our trains. Instead I am going to make a suggestion, a local one – local because I can talk intimately about it – but I have no doubt others with far greater knowledge than me could equally recount similar suggestions for their own area.

In Hampshire we have one railway facility blatantly under-used, one opportunity missed, and one that could be developed if the will were present. For the first I refer to the branch from Totton to Fawley. Opened in 1925, this line lost its passenger service in the 1960s but has survived due to the need to transport oil products from (and sometimes to) the refinery at Fawley. In addition, there is some movement to and from the Marchwood military port. Sadly most of the oil traffic has gone, movement by pipe the preferred choice nowadays, but while the rail traffic may all but have disappeared, the nearby A326 – the ONLY route from Fawley and Hythe to Southampton – is ever more strangled with road traffic. This is recognised by the council, but will they do anything about restoring the rail service to help alleviate the problem? You guessed it – no. A very high proportion of the traffic on the A326 commutes to and from Southampton, so the railway would indeed help, but it appears this is not a priority exercise. Excuses such as a rail path from Totton to Southampton are given, but with a will I am sure it could be made to work. So, please 'Mr Council' and 'Mr Rail Operator', get together, start talking seriously and take some action instead of continuing to make excuses why it cannot be made to work.

If the Fawley line is considered 'difficult', let me make a second suggestion and this time it is really easy, indeed not a sleeper need be relaid, not a penny need be spent, I refer to a connection from Andover to Southampton. 'Ah,' I hear you say, '... but that line closed (well the section between Andover and Romsey, nearly fifty years ago).' Yes it did, but with modern diesel units and the use of the Laverstock loop, why not a peak hour direct service from Andover calling only at Romsey and thence to Southampton? This would serve two purposes, firstly relieve commuter traffic on the overburdened road from Andover to Romsey while in addition provide a direct service to Southampton for students and workers – and there are many. Worth mentioning is that the replacement bus service provided to link Romsey and Andover when the trains were originally withdrawn, was discontinued years ago, meaning the present means of using public transport is a suggested Romsey–Winchester–Andover journey taking around ninety minutes – traffic and connections permitting. (It would be an interesting exercise to discover just how many of these alternative bus services provided when branch lines were closed actually do still survive. I can think of only a very few.)

Which brings me to my final suggestion, a direct rail service from Romsey to Winchester without the need for a reversal at Eastleigh. Setting the scene. Let me say that for some years South West trains evidently acknowledged that Romsey deserved a direct rail service as they laid on a bus connecting certain rail services at Winchester with a road connection to and from Romsey. For whatever reason, this ceased but a far better alternative would be to lay in a curve at Eastleigh so trains might avoid it by simply turning north – likely journey time in total circa fifteen minutes.

Proving a network and service to suit modern needs does not necessarily always involve reopening lines closed to all traffic decades earlier. The Victorians built lines to serve what was needed in their day. For years we have struggled to adapt a Victorian network for different twentieth and now twenty-first century needs, but a little thought, some limited adaptations, a desire to deliver a service as well as a profit and, most of all, a will to best utilise what is already present is something that will be repaid many times over.

Finally, I should also take the opportunity to mention a bit of business with the deliberate intention of ensuring that the correct story is recounted rather as sometimes occurs, distortion leading to unintended results. Readers will be aware that in May 2015 Noodle Books became part of Crecy Publishing Ltd, hopefully the change taking place without too many hiccups to readers of *SW*. Crecy has now expanded further by taking on Ian Allan Publishing, but NOT I hasten to add the Ian Allan company, which continues to flourish in its different areas. Books previously published by Ian Allan will now be sold and distributed by Crecy, although the Ian Allan name will slowly disappear off the bookshelves. New titles and any future reprints of former IA titles will subsequently appear under a new name. Ian Allan had also been the owner of the 'OPC' – the Oxford Publishing Company – and this name will remain but now under the control of Crecy, indeed the range will be expanded. Many will know I had been involved with IA for some years but as from 1 January I will now be working solely for Crecy, continuing with *SW* as well as acting in a similar role to my position with IA. We have some interesting ideas, including a number of Southern-related titles, some new and others transferred from IA to Crecy. I look forward to announcing details very shortly – the first likely in the July issue of *SW*.

Kevin Robertson

Southern Loco Performance During the 1948 Locomotive Exchanges

Jeremy Clarke

At a time when we are fast approaching the fiftieth anniversary of the end of Southern steam it will also soon be seventy years to another anniversary, that of the start of the Locomotive Exchanges that followed Railway Nationalisation in 1948. Hence it may be an opportune time to look back at how Southern engines fared during this grand locomotive jamboree.

The proposals for national control of much of the country's passenger and freight transport systems had been laid out in the Labour Party 1945 election manifesto. But the Exchequer was effectively bankrupt and the UK only remained solvent as a result of a huge loan made jointly by the USA and Canada in July 1946. (This was not finally paid off until 2006.) As with the events post-First World War, the incoming Labour Government 'welshed' [though technically correct, the alternative 'welch' avoids causing any offence] on the agreements made with the railway companies for compensation and reward for their massive contribution to the war effort. In 1922 this failure to honour promises brought about the fudge of Grouping, when more than 160 different companies were drawn together into

the 'Big Four' with little thought about obvious boundaries; the ex-Great Central London–Manchester route for example, worked by the LNER, being sandwiched by LMS ex-Midland and former LNWR routes between the same two points.

By the same token, when the Government of 1945 came to consider the compensation due to shareholders of the Big Four, the attitude towards them was comparable, meaning the agreements made would not be kept. In the ungracious words of the Chancellor of the Exchequer, Dr Hugh Dalton, during the Parliamentary debate concerning their takeover by the state, the railways were described as '... a very poor bag of assets'. Of

Above and page 9:
Although the Southern Region had no locomotive type to submit for the freight trials, some of these started or ended at Eastleigh, whilst it is believed the other end of the test was Bristol. Here an ex-GWR 2-8-0 No 3805 is having the weight of the ash and clinker remaining in the firebox recorded, not an enviable task shovelling this out at the end of the test. Also seen at Eastleigh is ex-LNER O1 2-8-0 No 63789 but this time coupled to the former GWR dynamometer car and being made ready for a freight test to the Western Region via Salisbury. Other freight types involved in the tests were the LMS 8Fs and the Riddles design Austerity 2-8-0. (August 1948.)

course they were! They and their staff had been worked into the ground to keep the supply of men and munitions flowing, often under dangerous and disorganised conditions due to the enormous volumes of passengers and freight transported, the 'blackout', and the many inconvenient interruptions by the Luftwaffe. They were, not to put too fine a point on it, exhausted and by the Government's attitude, disgracefully unappreciated. That was not new of course. As John Bright – a great Parliamentarian, a brilliant orator and the President of the Board of Trade at the end of the 1860s – wrote, 'Railways have rendered more services and have received less gratitude than any other institution in the land.' Hear, hear! And unlike many Continental governments, the UK decided to invest very little of the millions of dollars received under the post-Second World War Marshall Plan in railway reconstruction.

So, to the delight of many and the concern of more than a few, British Railways came into being on 1 January 1948, though the last 'takeovers' were not completed until September that year.

Not much would change at the beginning. Other than company logos being suppressed in favour of 'British Railways' in full on tank or tender sides, plus the slow addition of 'Regional' prefixes to engine numbers and a rash of experimental liveries, the trains carried on much as before. However, now there was a unified Motive Power authority in being and plans were made to test various ex-'Big Four' engines over routes other than their own, ostensibly with a view to developing a 'standard' BR range from the results. Opinions on the reasons for and the needs for the tests vary, whilst justifiable questions were also raised about how expenditure in adding yet more locomotive designs to the hundreds already in existence could be justified in the light of existing economic conditions. The same question would continue to be asked for post-war orders of many engines, most of recent or updated 'Big Four' design, which continued to be filled up to 1950 and even beyond.

The most cynical answer perhaps is that the newly appointed Chief Mechanical Engineer, R. A. Riddles, who had supervised design and construction of the WD freight classes, was keen to leave a more obvious mark. Perhaps more realistically, having a standard range was seen as a means of attempting to integrate the past with the future, although in reality that would take much longer, especially on the ground where loyalty, if not always politics, was strongly entrenched. It is interesting also to speculate what might have happened had one of the four CMEs been offered the role that Riddles took … an A4 with an oil bath? Perhaps, if Mr Bulleid had been left in charge … the mind boggles.

In many respects, however, continuing with steam motive power was sensible. The steam engine was relatively cheap to build and the country still had rich supplies of good steam coal, though the best was now going for export to improve the Exchequer's financial condition. Moreover, the brief flirtation with oil-firing in 1947 had shown how the Treasury soon ran out of the necessary dollars to purchase locomotive fuel in quantity, especially as demand (and thus price) rose. (Sterling,

at $4.86/£1 in 1939, had been devalued by 17 per cent to $4.03 under the Bretton Woods agreement of 1940. By 1949 this had proved unsustainable and a further devaluation of no less than 30.5 per cent, a condition of the loan from the USA, saw the rate pegged at $2.80. Further devaluation by another 14 per cent in November 1967 took sterling to $2.40.)

At nationalisation there were forty-nine diesel shunters of various designs on Britain's railways, and just one mainline diesel-electric locomotive, the LMS No 10000. (Sister engine No 10001 followed a few weeks into 1948.) Major investment in this form of motive power was also out of the question for the time being, except for small shunting units, for the same reason as the abortive oil-firing of steam engines. The investment made in 1947 in modifying locomotives to burn oil and purchasing and erecting the necessary equipment thus had to be written off by the railway companies to their disadvantage. Only when the products emanating from the 1955 'Modernisation Plan' started to come on stream in the later 1950s did the major shift to diesel power begin and in hindsight it is plain to see how poorly this was managed. But these reasons of themselves could surely not justify a whole range of new steam designs being proposed. On the other hand, deferment of the most obvious course, widespread investment in electrification, the ideal motive power, was hardly surprising in a country bankrupted by war.

So steam it was to be, but complete unification of motive power was seen by the new British Transport Commission as the ideal. Thus, between April and September 1948 a series of tests was run with locomotives over several different routes and principally in three categories, Express Passenger, General Purpose and Heavy Freight, with the view to cherry-pick the most desirable aspects of existing designs to form new builds. Competitive testing was not new of course, the earliest recorded being in 1870 between a LSWR Beattie Centaur class 2-4-0 and a SER Cudworth Single, principally to determine the relative efficiency of burning coal in their respective 'patent' fireboxes. The results are elusive!

Probably the most notable comparison concerned the 1925 exchange between a Collett Castle and a Gresley A1, which followed the British Empire Exhibition of 1924. The pioneer *Caerphilly Castle*, noticeably the smaller as it stood side-by-side with *Flying Scotsman*, was advertised by the GWR as the 'most powerful engine' in Britain on the basis of that most deceptive of yardsticks, tractive effort. This was in effect throwing down a gauntlet and Gresley rose to the challenge 'Prove it' he might have said to Collett at Swindon. He did!*As a result, alterations to lengthen the valve travel of the LNER A1 type reduced coal consumption from an average of 50lb per mile to 38lb, and, taken together with the introduction of a higher pressure boiler and modified cylinders, ushered in the immortal A3. But I ask again, was all the ballyhoo of 1948 really necessary? I think not, for in 1937 the LMS and LNER had decided jointly to fund and build a testing plant at Rugby. Neither the GWR nor the Southern expressed an interest, the one already having its own testing facility at Swindon, the other concentrating on an ongoing electrification programme.

The Rugby proposal had followed an earlier one made in 1927 by Gresley for a similar installation at Leeds, when it was hoped some Government funding might be forthcoming. However, the financial situation that developed at the end of that decade saw Government support refused and the scheme dropped in 1930. Later, however, and buoyed by the country's generally improving financial situation, work at Rugby resumed late in 1938, the 1933-built testing station at Vitry in France, and the Pennsylvania Railroad's Altoona plant both providing some design ideas. Not surprisingly the outbreak of war halted progress, and Rugby was finally commissioning in October 1948, a month after the Locomotive Exchanges had been completed. It must have been clear even as the Big Four were drawing their last corporate collective breaths that this plant would be 'on line' within the year. Scientifically controlled testing there and properly conducted trials 'on the road' would in time yield far more meaningful and useful data than ever came out of the Exchange Trials. But it could never be the same as 'boys playing trains on the main line'.

A further question about the necessity of the Standard type also arises. It was soon clear that with former LMS men dominating BR's motive power offices – Riddles himself was Crewe-trained and naturally, as the boss, picked many of his team – that company's practices were most likely to predominate irrespective of the outcome of the Trials. Was the whole thing then simply a charade, Riddles considering it a sop to the Mechanical Engineers of the other companies who retained their posts *pro tem* knowing, or at least suspecting, their contributions would be minimal? Perhaps I do him a disservice but that was very nearly the ultimate result when the 'Standard' designs were decided upon and produced. E. S. Cox – another LMS man who took up a premium apprenticeship at Horwich in 1917 – summed this up well when he wrote, 'It so happens that *in certain cases* (my italics) LM designs have the highest route availability for their power, and at the same time incorporate the latest advances in design from an operating and maintenance point of view.' Hmm! Who could forget the original Ivatt 4MTs, whose steaming abilities were put to shame almost by the ordinary kitchen kettle? But then the nail is driven in, '…. and the latest SR engines do not provide the requirements of simplicity and ease of maintenance which is the cornerstone of the present scheme'. Hmm again! But then did nobody in authority ever look at a later Arthur, in Derek Cross's opinion the Southern's answer to the LMS Black 5 and a better one too, or a Maunsell Mogul? Neither was that modern I agree but surely had other explicit qualifications! Apparently not. Having said all that, it was a former Southern Railway man, C. S. Cocks, who went from Brighton to Derby to take charge of design under Riddles and Cox. *(C. S. Cocks had come to Brighton from the LNER during the early part of Bulleid's tenure, NOT as has been previously recorded by accompanying Bulleid at the time of his own move. More simply this was a desire by Cocks to move south following a family holiday in the area. According to J. G. Click, following Cocks' holiday, he wrote to the Southern enquiring as to any vacancies. Nothing was heard for some time but then when Bulleid arrived at Brighton, the application was either shown to – or found by – Bulleid. The rest, as they say, is history. Ed.)*

The Southern's contribution to the tests consisted of Bulleid Pacifics of both types to compete – though that was a word never used in this context – in the Express Passenger and General Purpose categories. Having no designated locos in the heavy freight category, the SR took no part. (An ER 2-8-0 was later tried between Salisbury and Eastleigh, successfully perhaps, but ultimately unnecessarily.)

The specified requirement for all the engines was that they had run between 20,000 and 30,000 miles since the last general overhaul, which ensured they were well run in but still fresh enough to minimise the possibility of failure away from 'home ground'. Crew selection also proved critical, at least so far as the Southern was concerned, and for some time beforehand senior enginemen found themselves coming under unusually frequent attention from Locomotive Inspectors. Two firemen and four drivers were ultimately chosen. Two of the four, Jack Gilmore and George Robjant, were to act as conductors for the 'foreign' crews, the latter also being 'standby' in the event of a selected 'away' driver being unable to take duty. The 'away' crews were Driver George James and Fireman George Reynolds, and Driver Jack Swain with Fireman A. E. 'Bert' Hooker. It may be noted all these men were based at Nine Elms and they were probably as well fitted for the job as any, since neither the Eastern nor Central Divisions of the SR could readily muster journeys as long as those regularly undertaken by crews on the Western Division. Even a Kent 'rounder' did not form one continuous journey.

At this time the Southern double-manned many of its main line engines. Three of the men selected, Driver James and Firemen Reynolds and Hooker, were all from 21C20 *Bibby Line*, though that engine did not feature in the tests. Instead, those selected for the Express Passenger trials were Nos 35017 *Belgian Marine,* and 35019 *French Line CGT*. These were from the second batch of ten built at Eastleigh to order HO1189, appearing in April and June 1945 respectively. Messrs James and Reynolds worked Paddington–Plymouth with No 35019 and also manned No 35017 between Kings Cross and Leeds: Messrs Swain and Hooker took No 35017 engine over the Euston–Carlisle route. For the General Purpose tests the Southern selected West Country class Nos 34004, *Yeovil*, 34005, *Barnstaple* and 34006, *Bude*. These too were from 1945, all three coming into service from Brighton (order No 2421) in July. James and Reynolds took No 34005 between St Pancras and Manchester and No 34006 on Bristol–Plymouth runs. Swain and Hooker had the latter engine between Marylebone and Manchester and 34004 over the former Highland Railway Perth–Inverness route. The same engine had originally been booked to work the trials on the Great Central line but did not do so as following a light-engine trip two days before going to Neasden, mainly to see if any minor matters needed attention, some superheater flues were found to be leaking badly. It appeared they had not been 'rolled' properly following replacement and renewal of the elements. No 34006 *Bude* was therefore sent instead.

Being built for the relatively short distances run on the Southern, the tenders were exchanged for the LMS Black 5-type

holding 9 tons of coal but only 4,000 gallons of water. Use of the pick-up apparatus had thus to be mastered. Fireman Bert Hooker recalls he was disappointed to find the coal space was not self-trimming as in the Bulleid tenders and many of those then attached to Maunsell engines. Moreover, the shovelling plate was at least 6in lower than that of the MN. The upshot was that for the first 50 or 60 miles of a trip the coal continually fell off the plate through the large gap under the doors and had thus to be fired off the floor. Things then became more manageable, though again coal had to be lifted, this time from the shovelling plate to the firehole door. Finally, in the latter stages, perhaps for the last 80 miles or more of the run to Carlisle for example, the fireman had to enter the tender to pull coal forward, a rather tiring exercise after several hours work. (For tests on the Waterloo–Exeter route the ex-LMS engines were provided with WD-type eight-wheel 5,000-gallon tenders of which more later.)

Those test engines selected from other Regions in the Express Passenger category were: A4 and Duchess Pacifics, and King and rebuilt Royal Scot 4-6-0s. General Purpose representatives were Hall, Black 5 and B1 4-6-0s. In some respects the selections were questionable, the West Country for example being power classified 7P/5F against 5MT of the others in its category. And why did Doncaster go for A4s at least 10 years old rather than the latest Peppercorn A2s, particularly knowing the potential weakness of the Gresley derived valve motion, twice a failure during the tests? (The first of the splendid Peppercorn A1s was not outshopped until August that year.)

I am still rather disappointed that what one might call 'second rank' engines did not appear: a V2, a Castle, a Jubilee perhaps and a Lord Nelson for example. It would have been interesting to see how a Nelson with Bulleid's modifications would have fared given its doubtful reputation. But with an experienced crew and Stephen Townroe's preparation, who could tell? As it turned out the Scot in the Express Passenger category was arguably the star of the show. Were Maunsell's shades rather amused at the thought Fowler's draughtsmen had laid out the original with a full set of Nelson drawings at their elbows? In 1943 Stanier had started putting on new taper boilers, the three Scots taking part in the tests being thus equipped. The trials might also be assessed as incomplete, loading gauge limits prohibiting GWR engines from running over Southern metals whilst other than on its home turf the King was only permitted between Kings Cross and Leeds. The Hall was similarly limited to the Great Central route.

Various experienced travelling timekeepers 'logged' some of the test runs and that doyen of journalist/railwayman, Cecil J. Allen, published a book containing a fairly comprehensive, though inevitably incomplete, collection of them, including his own. Obviously expecting every run to be timed by people other than the staff manning the dynamometer cars is an impossible ask since more than one test could be run on the same day and the majority of the 'amateurs' were in full-time employment. Allen also pointed out that when the book appeared in 1949 no data in the freight engine category had

been released, though his follow-up publication contained a resumé of all the results published by the Railway Executive.

We are more fortunate in having the human side of the event from the estimable Bert Hooker. In that regard Allen could be fallible as, for example, when commenting on a LCGB Special out of Waterloo headed by A4 no 60022, *Mallard,* in January 1963. Approaching Byfleet (by now) driver Hooker noticed the water had got very high in the glass. Wary lest priming should occur he partly closed the regulator until the level had fallen back a little. Allen noted in his record of the run published in *Trains Illustrated,* 'The engine was unaccountably eased at Byfleet' though he obviously made no effort to find out why as there certainly was 'account'. AEH leaves us to draw our own conclusions. As if to emphasise how his opinions should not always be taken at face value, Allen provides a rather devastating account of a trip on a Billinton Baltic 4-6-4 tank engine in 1922. Three miles out from Brighton, '… the driver fixed his cut off at 35 per cent and regulator at ⅗ open. Thence he never touched either, uphill or down dale, until a slight signal check at Purley compelled action … about the most unenterprising bit of locomotive handling that it has been my lot to witness'. But as one commentator later said, would he have written so adversely had he timed the trip from the train rather than from the footplate? The 350-ton *Southern Belle* was being run nicely to time until that check, and the long but relatively easy rises and falls of the Brighton Line did not require constant attention to the controls or, indeed, to the fire. As it was, signals checked the train until East Croydon but the driver still made Victoria on time. The fact Allen makes no comment on the still punctual arrival leaves one to draw one's own conclusions. This is not to decry his presentation of the facts as known, nor his general assessments of the trips, merely that experience tells us some care ought perhaps to be taken in accepting some of his comments and opinions at face value.

Having said that, he questions why a particular driver, someone he had almost always found very dull and *unenterprising* – that word again! – in his work, was chosen to run the A1 Pacific on home ground in 1925 in competition with No 4079 *Pendennis Castle,* in the hands of the imperturbable and very experienced driver Albert Young of Old Oak Common. Coincidentally, he voices the same opinion on the nameless SR man whose running on home soil apparently compared poorly with that of his colleagues in the away team; and by the way, in his primary book on the Exchanges, Allen deliberately shows no detailed records of any 'home ground' runs, justifying this by saying that such work could be seen every day anyway and it was thus pointless losing limited opportunities to travel with the 'away' crews, though he does occasionally draw comparisons. *(Worth mentioning is that at the time railway publishers were nowhere near as prolific as in recent years. [Was paper rationing still in place at that time?] Nowadays it is right that we question authors and if necessary give forth opinion and/or correction. Seventy years ago the culture was more likely to accept without question. – Ed.)*

Every crew was given three days in the week prior to the tests to gain at least some experience and familiarity with each route by working over it on normal service trains. They were also accompanied by an inspector from their own Region, though he usually rode in the train rather than on the footplate. Allen comments that foreign engines working over the Southern probably put up the most consistent performances because only two men acted as pilots. From Hooker's account it appears he and Jack Swain were usually in the care of the crew that would have taken the turn, though the fireman would sometimes cede his place on the footplate to a member of the dynamometer car team and ride in the train. The visitors and indeed management, might well have hoped the home crew would pass on useful tips to the visitors. Perhaps this did not always take place for the simple reason of company loyalty and not wishing to see their own efforts or home-grown engines usurped by the interlopers. Considering the hierarchical structure of the footplate, it would also not have been the done thing for a visiting fireman to ask questions of a local driver. Hooker and his colleagues could therefore have been said to have started the trials at a distinct disadvantage. Even so, it should also be said that a footplate with a minimum of four, on occasion five, men present could lead to overcrowding in certain areas, so for one man to give up his place for train is also understandable.

In view of its specific fame it is not surprising the LNER selected No 22 Mallard (by then renumbered on paper at least as BR No 60022) to represent their honour in the express passenger category. Unfortunately though it was subsequently found to be a bad choice because, whilst No 22 commenced the trials on the SR, it subsequently failed and was replaced on both the Southern and later the Western Region trials by sister engine No 60033 Seagull. In company with a Lord Nelson and the products of an earlier era, Mallard reposes outside Nine Elms depot on 2 June 1948.

At the head of its first Waterloo–Exeter working, Mallard departs Waterloo on 8 June 1948 attached to the (G)WR dynamometer car and the usual rake of passenger coaches for the service. Not surprisingly the stranger has created much interest.

Obviously, in those circumstances, without the uniform style of driving imposed on French footplate crews for example, a driver's particular way of doing things would impinge directly on his piloting advice, which could also be dependent on how well he took to instructing others. One other point to make clear. Bert Hooker is adamant that he and his colleagues received no advice or instruction on how their engines should be driven and fired. And he is equally adamant that Southern crews away from home were keen to show what their engines could do. This contrasts with the attitude of some other 'contestants' who appeared to favour fuel economy over timekeeping or, more particularly, making up any lost time. To a degree, the attitude of the Southern men is a reflection of the SR's vigorously pursued 'on time' philosophy, essential when it ran the world's most intensive electric suburban service. As a

further illustration of this, E. S. Beavor, sometime shedmaster at Exmouth Junction, maintained his family home in Exeter following a promotion that took him back to London. He comments that in 1960 and for part of 1961 he would regularly travel back to Devon on a Friday evening by the 5.30pm from Paddington, The Mayflower. That train rarely arrived in Exeter on time, averaging about thirty minutes late, sometimes twice that, usually without apparent cause. He writes, 'It was my impression that either there was a deplorable lack of effort on the part of the enginemen or that some of them were repeatedly manufacturing overtime.' Though an LNER-trained man, he took wholeheartedly to the Southern's rigorous follow-up of 'lost-time' tickets, which is clearly why he deplored the lackadaisical running on his Friday evening journeys of what the WR authorities obviously considered a 'premier service', though apparently failing to check it was being run like one. But then for years the SR circulated each month a sort of 'league table' showing comparative running performances of the various depots. To a degree it was competitive, though Beavor admits Exmouth Junction, by virtue of much of its allocation being out-shedded at rural locations with comparatively sparse traffic and, in the main, somewhat undemanding timetables, usually came well up the league. This is not to imply the crews of Western engines taking part in the trials did not always do their best, though to a degree they were handicapped by firing hard Yorkshire coal in line with all the other participants, rather than their favoured soft Welsh. I merely point out that Southern men had the necessity for good timekeeping imbued in them from their earliest days on the footplate.

Before getting into the 'nitty-gritty' it may be worth reminding ourselves how far the railways have advanced in terms of speed in the intervening years. Throughout the recording of events there is a sense of real achievement in point-to-point averages of, say, 55mph, or hill-climbing sustained at 45mph, or even maxima into the 70s, such things being considered worthy of sometimes effusive praise. It may also be worth noting that the highest 'equivalent drawbar horsepower' recorded in the tests was 2,010 by none other than the Southern West Country *Bude* heading south out of Leicester following a call from the dynamometer car to 'give us a pull Jack'. In fact, this engine recorded two of the three

highest outputs noted for all the engines. But think too how much effort into gaining such output compares with what is available nowadays at the flick of a switch or the movement of a control handle. One final point: loads were substantial by today's standards though not uncommon up to that time. So much then, for the *Hors d'oeuvre* and on to the *Entree*!

From the operating point of view, the West Coast main line between Euston and Carlisle was the one most plagued by speed restrictions for permanent way and other maintenance work and consequent signal checks. Perhaps for this reason, in his reporting of journeys over this route Allen tends mainly to summarise the test runs rather than fully log them. Thus, as workings here are among the least documented it seems best to discuss their running first.

Bert Hooker describes the apprehension he and his colleague Jack Swain and, no less, the Southern's travelling inspector, the popular and much respected Danny Knight, who accompanied them, felt at tackling this route. After all, the distance of 299 miles was well over twice that of the longest they'd ever make on the Southern. In general at this time trains on the London–Weymouth run – 142¾ miles – were re-manned at Bournemouth – 108 miles – if the engine was working 'through'. Nine Elms men on Exeter or Plymouth trains were relieved at Salisbury, 83½ miles from London, and if the MN on the Atlantic Coast Express for example was working right down to Exeter the distance was still only 171.4 miles.

No 35017 on a familiarisation run prior to the full-scale trials. The train is the 10.00 from Euston and was recorded passing Berkhamstead – by H. C. Casserley of course! – the location being the photographer's home station having moved from Bromley to Berkshampstead in 1939.

13 May 1948, the first day of the trials proper for No 35017 from Euston. Behind the tender are no fewer than sixteen bogie vehicles weighing 530 tons, the first being the ex L & Y dynamometer car. The train is the down Royal Scot passing Bushey troughs. Jack Swain and Bert Hooker are in charge accompanied by an LMS pilotman and probably Inspector Danny Knight. Regrettably, no images showing the tests with the engine and train in the later stages of the run to Carlisle have been located.

Having then had their three days 'practice', on 13 May Jack Swain took No 35017 out of Euston at the head of the 530 tons gross Royal Scot. (As part of the test no banking assistance was permitted up to Camden.) Barely into motion, *Belgian Marine* was brought to a stand by signals before entering Primrose Hill tunnel and was stopped again at Kilburn. Having then observed a 30mph pwr at Willesden, the train was already ten minutes late passing Watford, only 17 miles out. Further signal checks and pwr slowings meant the lateness had grown to seventeen minutes by the time *Belgian Marine* drew to a stand at Rugby. However, despite further slowings for track repairs at Tamworth and Lichfield, Swain kept the fifty-six-minute allowance to Stafford before meeting another pwr on the climb to Whitmore. But a steady acceleration to 59mph at the head of the climb and a maximum of 70½ at Betley Road brought the train into Crewe in just over 83½ minutes from Rugby, 6½ minutes less than schedule despite five out-of-course slowings.

North of Crewe, operating failures in addition to some severe speed restrictions conspired to make any attempt at timekeeping futile and invalidate much of the test recording. None of the 'foreign' engines involved kept the schedule of

183 minutes for the 141 miles from Crewe to Carlisle. Jack Swain made the most spirited run, perhaps because of the delays suffered to Crewe. Having arrived there eleven minutes late and stood for thirteen minutes, which included taking water, *Belgian Marine* suffered further delays of 5¾ minutes by more maintenance restrictions. But Swain gained 2¾ minutes on the 12 uphill miles between Carnforth and Oxenholme before being summarily checked there by signals and thus losing all impetus for the 7 miles at 1 in 124/131/106 up to Grayrigg. Allen reports the engine was not pressed too hard over this section, which meant it had plenty in hand for the steeper climb to Shap, taking only 9½ minutes from Tebay to the summit. He also comments that although speed at Tebay following the slack at Dillicar had risen only to 57½mph, it had fallen back to no further than 26½ at Scout Green, halfway up the 1 in 75, but then increased to 29mph when the engine was 'opened out'. In the course of the swift run onwards to Carlisle, No 35017 picked up eleven minutes, though five of those were marked 'recovery time'.

On a familiarisation run the previous week, the engine had to stop for water at Lancaster. The crew had already discovered the scoop picked up almost nothing at the troughs at Bushey and Castlethorpe. Water had been taken during stops at Rugby and Crewe, though again picking up at Moore and Brock troughs had been minimal. Bert Hooker reports because of the slow flow it took seventeen minutes to fill the tank and there appeared to be any number of tiddlers thrashing about in it! In that instance Swain made a grand climb to Grayrigg, covering the 26.2 miles in only 34½ minutes and continued on to Carlisle without taking any more water. (It transpired a shunter moving the engine at Nine Elms had mistaken the operating handle for that of the tender handbrake, the lowered scoop striking a brick pathway across the track and becoming thoroughly out of shape.)

Due to the slack-ridden state of the route and other test runs occurring at the same time over less troubled lines, Allen made only one southbound run from Carlisle, on 14 May, and that behind *Belgian Marine*. But, as he put it, 'I would not have missed this trip for worlds.' The previous evening, in the Upperby hostel, fireman Hooker had asked a top-link Crewe driver how fast a climb could be made from the Penrith start to Shap summit. On being told 'twenty-two or twenty-three minutes, not less', Bert had surmised No 35017 could achieve it in twenty minutes. The succinct reply was to the effect there wasn't an engine capable of doing that, if expressed perhaps in rather more colourful language.

The 525-ton gross load of the 'Up Perth' was taken over the 17.8 uphill miles from Citadel to Penrith in a minute over the thirty-one scheduled, though signals had twice all but stopped *Belgian Marine* in the approaches to the Cumbrian town. The first 3 miles out of Penrith are relatively easy, No 35017 attaining 46mph on the ¾-mile level before the 7 miles up through the Eden Valley at 1 in 125. Here, Allen states, '... we settled down to a steady 41mph, which continued unvaryingly for mile after mile ... Before reaching the end of the 1 in 125 the speed was beginning to rise: on the [following 1¼ miles at] 1 in 142 we attained 46mph and the Shap level [station] carried the rate up to 51mph. By the end of the 1 in 125 ... the engine was exerting fully 1,700hp at the drawbar continuously. A brief drop to 46mph on the final 1¼ miles up at 1 in 106/130 and we were passing the Summit cabin in one second over 20½ minutes from the dead start at Penrith – a gain of 6½ minutes on schedule!' (Some hyperbole deleted!)

The train was still six minutes ahead of time on passing Preston despite two temporary restrictions *en route,* which Allen reckoned cost three minutes in running. By Springs Branch (Wigan) *Belgian Marine* was running 11½ minutes early but there were no fewer than eight permanent way and signals checks to contend with before Crewe. These included a stand outside the station though arrival there was still 2½ minutes before time, No 35017 drawing up alongside a 'leave special'

Familiarisation run for No 35017, this time on the Eastern Region and taken in May 1948. The engine and train are leaving Hadley Wood tunnel with a down train to Leeds. The LMS tender attached to No 35017 was again required for the water troughs on the ER main line. *B. Whitworth*

carrying RAF personnel, the probable cause of adverse signals received in the approaches. But what followed nullified any of the following findings in the dynamometer car, for the 'special' was permitted to leave Crewe immediately ahead of *Belgian Marine.* The first signal check came after a mile, the second 3 miles further on. Allen comments very acidly that he saw no reason why the 'special' couldn't have been moved to the slow road before Stafford as they passed nothing on it in the intervening 13 miles. But not until Leighton Buzzard, 118 miles to the south, was that move made. No 35017 thus arrived at Euston forty minutes late which, Bert Hooker writes, was apparently in line with the 'Up Perth's usual record.

However, he adds another slant here. Having merely noted that 'the operating authorities ... really slipped up there', he adds that it crossed his mind the engine and crew perhaps did too well on their familiarisation runs, reason enough maybe to spoil their timely progress on this test trip. Does that perhaps lend weight to my earlier suggestion that LMR authorities already knew/surmised little would actually come of the tests simply because 'their team' was already in charge of locomotive development, so anything that might dent their certainty had to be discouraged? Or am I being unduly cynical?

On that rather sour note then to Kings Cross. Running on the East Coast line was handicapped by an overall speed restriction of 60mph out to Hatfield and 70mph thereafter in view of maintenance arrears still being made up, though there were fewer speed restrictions in force than faced crews out of Euston. Allen had no opportunity to ride behind *Belgian Marine* on northbound runs but he summarises one timed by a correspondent on Tuesday, 25 May. Permanent way slowings to Peterborough were observed at Wood Green, right at the foot of the 8 miles at 1 in 200 to the summit at Potters Bar, and at Connington at the bottom of the run down towards Peterborough from Abbotts Ripton. With a gross load estimated at 535 tons, No 35017 recovered to a steady 37½mph after the Wood Green check to pass Hatfield only ½-minute late and Hitchin (31m 74ch) on time. Speed did not exceed 68mph before Peterborough, reached in 90¼ minutes or about 85 net. The really interesting part followed, the climb to Stoke summit. Here comparisons are made with the work of the Royal Scot *Queen's Westminster Rifleman.* With a similar load and in the hands of the LMR's most enterprising driver, Brooker, the *Rifleman* started rather the faster, sustaining 61–62½ mph up the slightly undulating rise to Essendine, followed by a minimum of 48mph at Little Bytham, before falling only to 47mph on the final three miles at 1 in 178 to Stoke from an intermediate recovery to 53mph at Corby Glen. By comparison, and despite the slower start, George James got to 65mph before Essendine, though passing through the station itself at 61mph and then accelerating to 63mph before falling back to 47mph at Little Bytham. As with the Scot, there was a recovery at Corby Glen, to 55mph, but then speed fell only to 50mph at the summit. Allen summarises the times as 6min 13sec (4-6-0) and 6min 40sec (4-6-2) to Werrington Junction (3.1m), 15min 17sec and 15min 29sec to Essendine (12.2m), 24min 52sec and 25min 0sec to Corby Glen (20.7m), and 28min 34sec and 28min 26sec to Stoke (23.7m). Rightly, in view of its smaller size, Allen balances this run in the Scot's favour. Grantham incidentally

(29.1m), was reached in 34min 49sec and 34min 56sec respectively, a gain of three minutes on schedule. For further comparison, *City of Bradford* ran to time in 37min 39sec but *King Henry VI,* despite making a typically smart Western start, suffered two signal checks and exceeded the time allowance by three minutes, though the net time was calculated at a minute less than schedule. There is no further mention of *Belgian Marine's* work so one has to assume the correspondent left the train at Grantham.

Allen made a southward journey behind each of the four engines with the 7.50am Leeds–Kings Cross, 35017 featuring on 28 May. One particular oddity: Holbeck was the first stop, barely ½ mile from the start. Three minutes were allowed for that ½ mile but CJA remarks that with two minutes stand time there, the departures were all 1–1½ minutes earlier than the public timetable. The normal nine-coach load out of Leeds was augmented by four more vehicles from Bradford at Wakefield, one from York at Doncaster and another from Lincoln at Grantham. In the case of *Belgian Marine*, the gross tonnage increased from 320 to 455, 495 and 535. The Scot on Allen's trip was the most heavily laden of the four because the train was packed with supporters going to the Rugby League Cup Final at Wembley: from Grantham it hauled an estimated 545 tons.

The start from Holbeck is a difficult one, uphill at 1 in 50 for a half-mile followed by a short respite before the three miles at 1 in 100 to Ardsley. No 35017 tied with the 'King' in a few seconds over eleven minutes, cutting all but a minute off the allowance from Holbeck, but then drew slightly ahead before being stopped by signals outside Wakefield. This occurred on every one of Allen's trips while the Bradford portion was drawn clear before attachment. He tartly remarks the 7.50 could have left Leeds ten minutes later and still picked up the existing schedule at Grantham without any real effort being demanded. As it was No 35017 exceeded the twenty-one minute allowance to Wakefield by fifteen seconds, though Allen calculates the net at only 16½ minutes for the 9.9 miles.

Belgian Marine attained 48mph on the 1.7 miles to Sandal and fell away only to 40mph at the head of the subsequent climb at 1 in 150, passing mp 169¾ (6.1miles) in 9½ minutes, more than a minute faster than the Scot and the King and 1½ minutes quicker than the Duchess. It is virtually all downhill thereafter to Doncaster, No 35017 attaining a maximum of 72½mph before a signal check outside the station. Nevertheless, James cut the twenty-six-minute allowance from Wakefield by 1¼ minutes, the only one of the four to better the schedule, though Byford on the Duchess may just have done so but for a similar check on the approaches

Only the Scot failed to keep the twenty-four-minute booking to Retford, though of the four the Duchess alone had an unchecked run, in twenty-two minutes. Allen, however, credits the King with that time net, attained mainly because of driver Russell's smart running over the latter part of the section. The MN was assessed as taking ½ minutes longer and the Scot 24¼ minutes. The forty-four minutes allowed on to Grantham proved more than adequate, though signals again checked three of the trains on the approach, the King on this occasion being the beneficiary. The Scot made the fastest time, of 40¼ minutes (net 38½), but only by dint of an excessive 77½mph on the descent from Askham tunnel through The Dukeries, though Allen nevertheless comments that rain and mist made rail conditions difficult. Despite the check, James, with 35017, cut the timing by 2¾ minutes, although he was credited with the same net time as the Scot.

The train was now non-stop to Kings Cross on a schedule of 122 minutes for the 105½ miles. James made the fastest climb to Stoke in an outstanding time of 9min 37sec for the 5.4 miles at 1 in 200 from the start, passing the summit box at 46mph. Allen comments that he believed the record had been set by the King a week previously in a time of 10min 8sec, and went on to say he had not discovered among his records such a fast start with a comparably loaded LNER engine as put up by the MN. (His further, more considered perusal shows that three A4s and a Gresley A1 had in fact bettered it but by a matter of seconds only. However, the rebuilt 'hush-hush' engine beat it by ¾ minute!)

Then, having attained 70½mph by Corby Glen, James eased the engine for the rest of the run down Stoke bank until the speed had fallen away to about 55mph, where normally trains would be travelling at 70. As there appeared to be no signalling responsible for this, CJA wonders if it may have been due to caution by the pilotman, particularly as Russell had also eased *King Henry VI* through Essendine without apparent cause, possibly with the same man on his footplate. Nevertheless, No 35017 was through Peterborough 1¾ minutes ahead of time. The King was marginally quicker, having been a ½ minute behind at Stoke box but making a faster run along the level through Werrington Junction.

In typical Western fashion, the King made a smarter recovery from the 20mph limit through Peterborough North station but *Belgian Marine* climbed strongly to Abbotts Ripton to pass Huntingdon a minute early and forty seconds ahead of *King Henry VI*. Thereafter, the two ran within seconds of each other until No 6018 was twice checked by signals, slight at Potters Bar – taking not quite ½ minute more than 35017 from Hatfield – but a little more harshly at New Barnet on the run down into London. Thus James was through Wood Green more than three minutes ahead of Russell though both had to observe a pwr at Finsbury Park. It is apparent from the few intermediate timings shown, both drivers had been intent on getting a little time in hand to compensate for this. No 6018 then had a clear run into Kings Cross but 35017 was checked to walking pace at Belle Isle though still arriving 1¾ minutes before time: the King was a minute early.

In the meantime, Driver Brooker with the Scot averaged a mile a minute from Stoke to Stevenage after observing a slack at Corby Glen and the permanent slowing through Peterborough North, taken at 22mph. The *Rifleman* went through Huntingdon at 77½mph – the second time on the trip that speed had been reached – and took only 25½ minutes for the 27 miles thence to Hichin, by which time Brooker was back on schedule.

Neither LMS engine had had to observe the pwr at Finsbury Park, and though *City of Bradford* received a slight signal check at Belle Isle, Byford arrived in 118¾ minutes from Grantham. Brooker also got in early, by 1¾ minutes, but Allen credits his engine with the fastest net time, 113¾ minutes. The Duchess is accorded a net of 114¼, the King 116 and *Belgian Marine* 117 minutes. I think this a little ungenerous considering the signal check at the close meant the last 2½ miles from Finsbury Park took no less than 7½ minutes, against the 3½ minutes of the King. I'd cut this 'net' figure by ½ minute and perhaps a bit more because James lost only a single minute on the seventeen allowed from Potters Bar, the pwr to 31mph and the severe signal check notwithstanding. (And Brooker twice grossly exceeded the 70mph overall line speed limit!)

This was an altogether happier event for James and Reynolds than Swain and Hooker experienced out of Euston though both crews acquitted themselves very well and certainly upheld the Southern tradition of attempting to run to time. Incidentally, Hooker tells of a conversation overheard by Inspector Knight between two sets of Crewe enginemen 'travelling home' who joined him at Rugby in the front brake van on one of the Royal Scot trips. One told his mates to '… get the cards out, this thing on the front [35017] will be an hour late into Crewe'. In fact, they had a good onward run, unchecked by signals, and got to Crewe eight minutes early. He also tells amusingly of the instruction by a Polmadie pilotman coming aboard at Crewe to 'fill up the firebox and fill the boiler' and who then got very agitated when Hooker, sitting quietly drinking a cup of tea, refused. 'After all, I knew *Belgian Marine* – he didn't!' He also had to restrain the fireman who had moved to pick up the shovel. The pilot crew was apparently astonished that after this slight disagreement the safety valves were sizzling as the train passed through Warrington. Then, having climbed Shap without trouble Swain was moved to ask the Scotsman, 'Where's this Shap summit we've heard so much about?' The reply said it all: 'Away! I'd give a week's money to take this engine through to Glasgow!'

So, now to move west. The Paddington–Plymouth test provided as much of a challenge for the crews in the Express Passenger category as it had presented to driver Albert Pibworth on the LNER A1 *Victor Wild* in 1925, though by this time both Westbury and Frome had been bypassed. (On the test runs Westbury was actually served) Other than the final 3 miles, the westward climb to the summit at Savernake is not particularly steep, but the 35-mile long and debilitating hike up the Kennet valley from Southcote Junction, and the 17-mile eastward climb from Lavington both abound in curves. In its way the Berks & Hants line is quite as difficult a proposition as the Devon banks. Other summits, at Brewham and particularly at Whiteball have steeper approaches and all three climbs require skilled handling from both sides of the footplate.

James and Reynolds crewed *French Line CGT* between London and Plymouth, the three Pacifics (Merchant Navy, A4, and Duchess types – not forgetting the 4-6-0 Scot) being required to handle loads of between 505 and 525 tons gross to Newton Abbot on the 1.30pm down. The Scot, with the enterprising Brooker again in charge, had the benefit of one

No 35019 French Line CGT attracts a similarly inquisitive audience at Paddington as it departs westwards on one of its own familiarisation runs. Other than when the the LNER sent an 'A1' to run from Paddington consequent upon the 1925 contest between the GWR and LNER, this would likely have been the first time a Pacific had been seen at Paddington since the days of Mr Churchward's Great Bear.

coach fewer, its train weighing 465 tons gross. It was the only engine Allen records to better the forty-five-minute schedule to Reading, though all four had exceeded the twenty-three-minute booking to Slough, the A4 *Seagull* by 2¼ minutes. But with twenty-two minutes allowed for the next 17½ miles to the Berkshire town, time might have been kept but for a pwr before Twyford that also affected No 35019 on the detailed trip of 27 April. James got in 1¼ minutes late while Burgess with No 60033 was a minute behind time. Byford and *City of Bradford* had made the best start but were still ½ minute late at Slough. However, a signal check to 25mph before Maidenhead hampered the run into Reading, making the Duchess 1½ minutes down also. Brooker meanwhile, untroubled after a pwr at Ealing Broadway came into Reading two minutes early.

Allen remarks that the seventy-minute allowance for the 59.6 miles to Westbury and particularly of only forty-two minutes for the 34.1 miles to Savernake requires rather more effort than that of the very easily graded first 36 miles. However, it is also rather puzzling that the downhill 25½ miles thence to Westbury are allowed twenty-eight minutes, curvature notwithstanding.

French Line CGT and *Queen's Westminster Rifleman* made the best starts from Reading, both gaining more than two minutes to Savernake, No 35019 sustaining a very respectable minimum of 45½mph over the final 3 miles at 1 in 175/183/145/106 to the summit. But a bad permanent way slowing to 18mph after Pewsey, which affected none of the other engines, spoiled the run to Westbury, though *French Line* had got up to 71½mph when passing Lavington at the foot of the descent. Allen reckons the net time for No 35019, actually arriving ¾ minute to the good, to be about 4½ minutes less than schedule. Meanwhile Brooker, again with *Queen's Westminster Rifleman*, seemed to suffer from an over-cautious pilotman, for not once on the descent to Westbury did he reach a mile a minute, but still got in 1¼ minutes early. By comparison Byford, with the Duchess, made a steady but timely ascent to Savernake and then forgot himself by providing an uncharacteristic display of the engine's capabilities, achieving 82mph at Lavington and arriving in 4¼ minutes less than the allowance. *Seagull* made a steady run without particular exertion going up or untoward speed coming down, contriving to arrive a minute under schedule.

Seen here in the unmistakable setting of Sonning cutting east of Reading, No 35019 heads west towards its eventual destination of Plymouth with the GWR dynamometer and what was a formal test. *Maurice Earley*

James made the smartest start from Westbury but still dropped 1½ minutes on the impossible seven-minute timing for the 4¾ miles to Clink Road Junction at Frome. Having sustained 47½mph to Brewham *French Line* passed through Castle Cary 'on the dot' at the prescribed limit of 60mph. Brooker on the Scot appeared still to be restrained by his pilotman, for a pedestrian 65mph at Bruton was followed by a slowing right down to 48mph for the Castle Cary slack. It is tempting to suppose the Western man did not want the 'foreigner' to do too well. More charitably, maybe he found the riding to his distaste: the Scots could get very rough as mileage built up but at the parameters set by the test that should not have been a factor here. Perhaps the man himself was overly cautious at the regulator, which on his 'home' engine would have been on the right side of the footplate, in both senses of the word to him. (Does this mean the pilotman was therefore driving the Scot?) As it was, Byford on the Duchess upheld LMS prestige by repeating his showing on Savernake at Brewham, topping the summit at 44mph but then coming down at a sprint, touching 77½ at Bruton and being checked only to 65mph through Castle Cary. As a result he was all but 1¼ minutes early at Creech Junction. *French Line* and *Seagull* both took ½ minute longer but Brooker, who had had to observe a pwr after Curry Rivel following the descent

from Somerton tunnel, was by now almost six minutes late passing the junction. All four engines were slowed by another pwr to 15mph before the stop at Taunton but No 35019 had managed to cut a bare ¼ minute off the fifty-three scheduled from Westbury. The A4 and Duchess were both on time but the Scot's lateness had increased to 6½ minutes.

James was the only driver to keep the sharp thirty-eight-minute booking net from Taunton to Exeter. The climb from Norton Fitzwarren to Whiteball begins quite easily but the 4 miles between Wellington and the summit at Whiteball siding includes 2½ miles at 1 in 90/86/80 before the easing to 1 in 127 through the fifty chains of the tunnel itself. With 505 tons on the drawbar No 35019 was making 50mph at Wellington (7.1m), entered the tunnel at 31mph and left it at exactly 30mph, covering the 10.9 miles from Taunton to summit in 17¼ minutes. The engine had accelerated to 75mph by Tiverton Junction, having been eased for the curves through Cullompton and Hele, and would have made Exeter in 36½ minutes but for an annoying slowing to walking pace by signals at Stoke Canon. The actual time was 40min 52sec to a stand at St David's. None of the other engines got to *French Line*'s pace at Wellington and all lost more than three minutes net to Exeter.

Even given the all-but level road, the timings between Exeter and Newton Abbot are demanding with the loads being hauled. Brooker with the Scot overturned things by being the only driver to better the sixteen minutes allowed to Dawlish, but only by rather overstepping the limit through Starcross. Allowing for delays demanded by pwr checks, James was the one driver to keep time to Newton, indeed Allen credits him with a gain of ¾ minute. The load was reduced here to 335 tons gross following detachment of the Torbay portion. The climb to Dainton begins a little less than 1½ miles from Newton Abbot but on the run recorded by Allen No 35019, observing a pwr to 27mph right at the foot at Aller Junction, gained very little impetus for it. Thus the engine lost 1¼ minutes on the eight-minute allowance to Dainton, passed at 25mph though accelerating from a minimum of 21½ over the slightly easier last ¼ mile. Despite the curving and speed-restricted run down to and through Totnes, James regained ½ minute before the 9-mile climb to Wrangaton. But for once *French Line* struggled, falling to 20½mph at Tigley (11½ miles from Newton) and topping Rattery a minute late. A further ½ minute was lost by Brent, though Allen calculates James to be just on the right side of time given the delay at Aller and not allowing for departure from Newton Abbot 1½ minutes ahead of the public timetable. A ¾ minute gain to Hemerdon siding and a swift run down the 1 in 42 from there, with a maximum of 69mph before Plympton, helped alleviate the effects of a 17mph pwr at Lipson Junction, James bringing the train into North Road at 6.55pm, on the dot of the advertised arrival time.

Eastbound runs were hampered from the start by a succession of restrictions between Plymouth and Newton Abbot such that timekeeping was impossible, the first, at Plym Bridge, near Tavistock Junction, being about 1½ miles from the foot of the climb to Hemerdon. Having observed this at 20mph on the return on 28 April, *French Line* had recovered to 42½mph before tackling the 1½ miles at 1 in 42. This time James made a very fine climb, speed falling to a minimum of only 17½mph at Hemerdon 'but not', according to Allen, 'appearing to be in any trouble at any point'. But for the check at Plym Bridge he estimates No 35019 would have passed the summit (6.7m) in fourteen minutes from the start rather than the 14½ minute schedule and the actual time of a few seconds over sixteen minutes.

This effort though was surpassed by *Seagull,* which had to come down to 16mph for a relaying slack in Plympton station itself. Speed then went up to 24mph on the short 1 in 111 immediately after it and had only fallen away to a very creditable 18½mph after the 1½ miles at 1 in 42 to Hemerdon, though by then the A4 was three minutes late. Only the Scot escaped any other permanent way checks, No 35019 having two in the 9½ miles between Hemerdon and Brent, the latter station being passed four minutes late. A minute had been recouped by Totnes, passed at a restricted 40mph. What followed was another excellent climb, taking only 7¼ minutes for the 4.9 miles to Dainton with speed being 23½mph at the summit. James was moderately checked by signals at Aller Junction and so brought his 350-ton train into Newton Abbot just over 2¼ minutes behind time though credited with a two-minute net gain on the fifty-one-minute schedule from Plymouth.

Allen remarks that the nine-minute allowance for attaching the Torbay portion ought to have been ample though it was exceeded in every case, *French Line CGT* being detained for no less than 13½ minutes. Departure with a load now of 525 tons gross was seven minutes late. But No 35019 was the only engine to make Exeter in the twenty-six minutes allowed (actually four seconds over!). Then, barely away from St David's, James was brought to a stand for four minutes by signals at Stoke Canon, losing all the impetus for the climb to Whiteball. Nevertheless, speed had fallen from 60mph at Cullompton only to 47½ at Burlescombe, almost at the head of the two miles at 1 in 115 that lead to the summit at Whiteball siding. Time recovery was hampered by yet another pw check just beyond the summit, arrival at Taunton thus being 4¼ minutes over the time allowed to be compounded by dilatory station work: James left Taunton nine minutes late.

Gradients are relatively easy for the next twenty-three miles or so but then comes the trying seven miles to Brewham, finishing with 1¾ miles at 1 in 98/81. *French Line* was over the top in thirty-eight minutes dead from the Taunton start at 35mph and gained 3½ minutes on the schedule to Westbury. Leaving there now only 6¼ minutes late, 35019 made an excellent climb to Savernake, passed at 55½mph, and thereby gained 2¾ minutes on the thirty-seven-minute allowance to Bedwyn. Signals slowed the train to 24mph before Kintbury but James was still through Newbury in ½ minute less than allowed.

The load was reduced by 40 tons on shedding the Reading slip coach, though passing through the platform loop there at 40mph provided for some lively riding. The last scheduled check, to 36mph at Twyford, was followed by a sprint for the terminus with maxima of 71½ at Slough and Ealing Broadway. Taking 105min 10sec from Westbury, James had brought his train into Paddington 1½ minutes before time. Allen estimated the net at 101 minutes, or twelve minutes less than schedule. He also calculates *French Line CGT* could have come up non-stop from Exeter, without delays, in a shade over three hours for the 173½ miles, an average of about 57½ mph.

While this was an excellent performance against the odds, it did not match that of the Scot over the latter section. For some reason Brooker had not done too well over the Devon banks or to Brewham and so got away from Westbury 14½ minutes behind time. Whatever his pilot driver may have advised, Brooker was clearly determined to salvage the reputation of himself and his engine. The start was as a shot from a gun with Pewsey passed at 70½mph and Savernake topped in only 27½ minutes at 50, the speed reduced to that from 69mph at Burbage siding for the curves. Another acceleration to 70½ at Kintbury preceded a 30mph pwr before Newbury, but Brooker was still through the station five minutes under schedule. Speed had recovered to 71½ before the slowing at Southcote junction in preparation for Reading.

Opposite: **Again attracting interesting after arrival back at Paddington with an up service from Plymouth – arrived 1.44 pm, 20 April 1948. Already the disc headcode has been changed from that of an Express Passenger working and a red tail lamp fitted above the left hand buffer, ready to run light to Old Oak Common.** *C. C. B. Herbert*

Such was the custom under the circumstances the train was then forced to stop rather than 'slip', being held in Reading's usual slothful fashion for all but three minutes, though arrival had been eight minutes under the scheduled passing time. But Brooker was away in almost a minute less from Westbury than it had taken James to pass through, and from the standing start the *Rifleman* had achieved all but 'even time' by Old Oak Common before a final pwr to 41mph at Westbourne Park. Allen puts the net time for this remarkable run at 96½ minutes, 16½ less than allowed though the train was actually into Paddington 6½ minutes down.

On that note let us turn to the working of *Bude* in the General Purpose category over much of the route just discussed. Nothing at all was recorded by Allen regarding any westbound workings from Bristol; neither, he comments, did he receive any correspondence on this from other timers. This is a pity, for it would have been very interesting to see how the GP engines would have handled the loads in this direction over Whiteball and the Devon banks. So we are restricted to looking at the Up times, which are, happily, well worth reiterating.

With a gross load of 260 tons from Plymouth *Bude* suffered the same 20mph pwr check before Plympton as all the Express engines, and was further checked through that station to 30mph at the foot of the climb to Hemerdon. As a result speed fell to 15½mph at the top of the 1 in 42, which together with a further pwr just over the summit, put the engine 3¼ minutes late at Brent. Another engineering restriction beyond that station hampered the possibility of any real time recovery down the grade to Totnes. The three miles to Dainton summit were completed in 6¾ minutes, a minute quicker than either the Black 5 or the B1, though speed had fallen to 16mph at the top. Restrained running around the curves down to Aller Junction precluded any recovery in the three-minute lateness being made before passing through Newton Abbot.

The story is taken up again with departure from Exeter St David's, the load being increased here to 449 tons net or about 475 tons gross. No 34006 seemed not to notice, the 19.9 miles to Whiteball being reeled off in 22¼ minutes start-to-pass, an average of 54mph. Speed had reached 68mph before the 60mph slack through Cullompton and rose again to 66½ at Tiverton Junction for the final assault through Burlescombe, where speed had fallen only to 53mph. No note is made of the rate at the summit itself as the engine was already braking for another pwr on the other side of Whiteball tunnel. However, 34006 went through Wellington at 76mph and came to rest at Taunton in 34min 53sec from St David's, the only engine bar one of the seven timed over this section – the Black 5– to better the thirty-eight minutes allowed. Allen calculates the net time as 33¾ minutes.

If this were a good showing, the run onward to Bristol produced some real fireworks. Having got to 55mph in the 2½ miles to Creech Junction speed rose rapidly to 73mph after Bridgwater and continued so along the level past Dunball, *Bude* achieving 'even time' by Highbridge, 17.9 miles from Taunton in 17min 37sec. The engine went over Flax Bourton summit at 70mph and then got to 75 through Long Ashton on the descent to Bristol. Such *joie de vivre* couldn't last, the train facing several signal checks before being brought to a stand at Temple Meads West box no less than eleven minutes early. It eventually drew into Temple Meads in 50¾ minutes against the fifty-three allowed. From Exeter, *Bude* had cut no less that 16½ minutes net off the ninety-three-minute timing. It is only fair to add that both the smaller engines coped well with the load. Driver Smith and the Black 5 made an unchecked run from Taunton to Bristol a minute faster than *Bude,* though No 45253 had been four minutes behind only a mile before Temple Meads. Similarly, driver Ratter and 'B1' No 61251 arrived in 2¼ minutes less than schedule despite two signal checks in the approaches, though they had been five minutes behind *Bude* at Flax Bourton. But in neither case could the net time match that put up by the Pacific. One oddity may be noted: the working timetable allowed two minutes more from Taunton than the public one.

So, from such rather tantalisingly scant but very satisfactory details from the Southern's point of view, back to London and the two routes to Manchester. CJA contends with some justification that, considering the loads hauled, the work out of Marylebone in particular was the hardest set the General Purpose engines.

Only the B1, Black 5 and West Country worked on the ex-Midland route. Like its West Coast counterpart, the southern part of the Midland line abounded in checks for track renewals. Allen himself did not make any runs out of St Pancras but reproduces those of another very experienced timer, though all start from and one finishes at Leicester. In all cases too the northbound workings set out late from Leicester due to the restrictions further south. The Southern's entrant in this instance was No 34005, *Barnstaple*, again crewed by the Georges, James and Reynolds, and the only one of the three that consistently kept sectional timings. The recorded northbound trip was made on 22 June with a gross load of 325 tons.

The start from Leicester is down the gentle slope of the Soar valley as the river heads for the Trent so, on the face of it, the timings noted ought to present few if any problems. Sixteen minutes are allowed for the 12½ miles to Loughborough, George James taking full advantage of this favourable road to pick up two minutes on the booking with a maximum of 70mph at Barrow-on-Soar. A further 2½ minutes were gained to Derby, 72mph having been reached at Kegworth before the 50mph slack for the curves at Trent Junction where the climb over the Pennines begins. This is easy for almost all the first 30 miles or so, though James dropped ½ minute to Matlock, mainly by being over-cautious through the curve at Ambergate. Time was just kept to Millers Dale despite a pwr at Rowsley, right at the foot of the 14 steep miles to Peak Forest. Except for three very short downhill sections the gradient is continuous, predominantly at 1 in 100, but it finishes with 3¼ miles at 1 in 90.

Following observation of the Rowsley restriction at 17mph, *Barnstaple* had accelerated to 42½mph by Headstone tunnel (6¼ miles) and then to 53mph in the following ½-mile dip. Speed fell back on the rise before the next dip, to Millers Dale, but only to 42mph. Ten minutes are allowed for the 4.6 miles

On another pre-trial familiarisation run, No 34005 Barnstaple awaits departure from St Pancras for Manchester on 14 June 1948. Messrs James and Reynolds are the likely ones seen leaning from the cab.

thence to Peak Forest, James cutting ¼ minute off this and making 64½mph once over the summit. The curve at Chapel-en-le-Frith demanded a slowing to 55mph and another pwr before Chinley brought speed down to 18mph. Despite these slacks James cut two minutes net off the twenty scheduled to this point from Millers Dale.

The final 19.7 miles into Manchester are steeply downhill as far as Cheadle Heath, passed at 72mph on the dot of the thirteen-minute allowance, before the usual slow run in from Chorlton Junction. *Barnstaple* reached the Central station ¼ minute under the twenty-five scheduled from Chinley and dead on time, the only one of the three recorded engines to do this. Allen estimates the net gain from Leicester at 8¾ minutes.

Heading south the following morning, *Barnstaple* departed with a gross load also of 325 tons. Allen's correspondent apparently did not join the train until its first stop, at Chinley, but some skeleton data were available. Cheadle Heath, right at the foot of the climb to Peak Forest, was passed ½ minute early at 60mph, rather faster than either of the 4-6-0s, and the engine sustained a minimum of 33½mph on the 1 in 87/89/90 to Chinley. Arrival here was no less than 4½ minutes before time. Getting away smartly again, No 34005 had accelerated

to 33mph up the 1 in 90 to Dove Holes, cutting two minutes off the fourteen allowed to Peak Forest. But the reduction in speed to 31½mph during passage of the near-1¾ miles of Dove Holes tunnel, which also rises at 1 in 90 for its entire length, suggests some easing of the regulator. The tunnel is driven through porous rock and is therefore wet, although there is no indication the engine suffered from slipping: the easing may then have been protective.

Following a quick burst at 60mph *Barnstaple* was slowed to 48 on the approach to Millers Dale but still came to rest there in a time of 17¾ minutes against a schedule of twenty-one. On the run down to Matlock a reduction in speed to 40mph was made at Hassop, 20mph less than either of the 4-6-0s, though the cause is not shown. That and the pwr at Rowsley and another to 13mph after Darley Dale brought no 34005 into Matlock in 2¾ minutes more than the sixteen allowed. Signals then spoiled a fast run into Derby, though time was kept.

Getting smartly away from Derby the 72mph recorded at Sawley came to an abrupt end with another signal stop of 3¾ minutes at Trent Junction, Loughborough thus being passed 4¾ minutes late at 72mph. Despite 70½ at Barrow-on-Soar and 66½ at Syston, *Barnstaple* was still a minute behind time into

Another view of No 34005 shortly after departing from St Pancras with the 10.15 am down train. Again this has to be a familiarisation/route learning duty as it is just an ordinary passenger vehicle that is coupled immediately behind the tender.

Leicester. Allen, however, estimates a net time of no more than 30½ minutes for the 29.4 miles from Derby, a gain of 6½ minutes on schedule. Both 4-6-0s had had a clear run and thus no need to hurry, the Black 5 – its 'homeground' working unusually being recorded – arriving 2¾ minutes early and the B1 1¼ minutes before time.

The continuation to St Pancras illustrates the effects of the engineering restrictions. No 34005 had barely left Leicester before a pwr reduced speed to 29mph. Although a further check to 28mph interfered with progress, James passed Market Harborough only ¼ minute down and then went over Desborough summit at 48mph after 3½ miles at 1 in 132. The run down to Wellingborough was spoiled by another pwr, this time before Kettering, to 26mph. Nevertheless, the train was through Wellingborough three minutes under schedule and James set about the climb to Sharnbrook with enough gusto to gain another minute at the summit, topping it at 47½ mph. PWRs either side of Bedford, to 17 and 30mph, provided incentive for another swift acceleration, up the long 1 in 200 gradient to Leagrave, cleared at 52½mph before a 68mph dash through Luton, six minutes ahead of time. With speed held in the high-sixties a further ½ minute had been acquired to St Albans despite the penultimate pwr of the trip, to 17mph on the approach. Hendon was passed at 74mph before the final slowing for engineering work, after Finchley Road, to 16mph. A signal check at Kentish Town spoiled the run into St Pancras, though *Barnstaple* came to rest in 115¾ minutes from

Leicester, 3¼ minutes early. Allen calculates No 34005 showed an overall net gain of no less than 29¾ minutes from Manchester, 16½ minutes of that from Leicester. It may be added the B1 acquitted itself very well: Allen calculated a net time of 111 minutes from Leicester against the schedule of 119, though it arrived ¾ minute late.

We move west along and beyond the Euston Road now to the quietest of all London termini, to take the ex-Great Central route to Manchester. As before the West Country, in this case no 34006 *Bude* crewed by Swain and Hooker, was rivalled by a Black 5, No 45253 again, but this time a Hall is included, the now-preserved No 6990, *Witherslack Hall*.

Bude's first recorded trip is northbound on 8 June with 380 tons gross. Allen notes the line out to Rickmansworth 'was crammed with permanent way restrictions' and track rearrangement in progress at Harrow. Nevertheless, despite checks to 18mph at Wembley Park and 5mph on the steep Harrow-on-the-Hill approaches, Swain had dropped less than ¾ minute on arrival there, mainly by virtue of a very fast start, Neasden South Junction, 5 miles from Marylebone, having been passed in 9¼ minutes at no less than 66mph. The restriction continued on leaving Harrow but then No 34006 faced a succession of signal checks culminating in a dead stand at Northwood Hills. That and a further pwr to 30mph contributed to the train passing Rickmansworth three minutes down. Undeterred, Swain made an excellent climb up the 6½ miles to Dutchlands summit, constantly at 1 in 105 other than

A final view of Barnstaple waiting to leave St Pancras – the signal gantry, signal box and even the position of the bridge girders having some similarity with the GWR station at Oxford.

Familiarisation runs for No 34006 Bude and crew from Marylebone on 31 May 1948. The engine and train (destined for Manchester but this time via the former Great Central route, are seen in the platform and also from track level about to pass an LNER L1 2-6-4T. *P. Ransome-Wallis and C. C. B. Herbert*

short levels through the stations at Chorleywood and Chalfont & Latimer, reaching 45mph at the top just beyond Amersham, and then falling away from 71½mph to only 60 on the subsequent 4 miles uphill through Great Missenden. There followed a 74mph dash through Wendover before another pwr, this time to 35mph, preceded arrival at Aylesbury 2¾ minutes over the allotted forty. Neither of the other engines came anywhere near this time, though neither had suffered a signal stop and the Hall had had a clear run this far.

There followed what Allen describes as a 'joyous sprint' when *Bude* achieved all but 'even-time' over the 31.2 miles to Woodford. Having got to 76½mph after Quainton Road, speed had to be reduced to 67 for Grendon Underwood Junction. Then, from 71½mph after Calvert the near-6 mile long rise through Finmere was topped at 59, followed by another swift acceleration in the short dip thereafter that saw Helmdon passed at 64mph. A final 69mph at Culworth Junction was enough to provide a Woodford arrival in 31min 24sec from Aylesbury against the schedule of thirty-five minutes. This works out at an average of 59.6mph start to stop over a generally rising road, most of those rises being at 1 in 176.

There was no 'fat' whatever in the seventeen-minute timing for the 14.1 miles to Rugby, though Swain may just have made it but for a 30mph pwr before the station. The maximum

on this section was 76½mph at Braunston, at the foot of the 6½ miles downgrade at 1 in 176 from the south end of Catesby tunnel. Allen estimates the net at sixteen minutes against *Bude's* actual 18½. The continuation on to Leicester saw Swain cut a few seconds short of three minutes off the twenty-three allowed for the 19.9 miles, another 59mph+ average, with a maximum of 75mph at Ashby Magna before the engine was eased at Whetstone. More significantly, No 34006 had gained most of those three minutes on the uphill 1 in 176 grades either side of Lutterworth.

Bude kept exact time on the tight allowance of twelve minutes to Loughborough but despite a fine acceleration away from there at 53mph to Barnston tunnel, a long slowing to 35mph because of pitfall meant the seventeen-minute allowance to Nottingham Victoria was exceeded by two minutes. It is worth noting that Bert Hooker said he found the ex-GCR line 'a lovely railway', with sweeping curves and long gradients. Certainly the later-built section south of Annesley – the true 'Great Central' – could be so described but north of there the old MS&LR was into mining country and from Sheffield faced the long and steep climb over the Pennines.

Bude left Nottingham on time and proceeded to give yet another demonstration of the hill-climbing ability of the Bulleid Pacifics. The gradient is rising almost continuously at 1 in

This time one of the pre-trial runs has been recorded near Northwood on what was the Metropolitan and Great Central joint lines – hence the conductor rails. Not mentioned within the text is the fact that the Southern crews would have been familiar with the working of steam over electrified lines, something of which the GW men on their Hall class engine had no experience. *J. C. Flemens*

130/132 for 11 miles to Kirby South Junction, but it starts with the damp Mansfield Road and Sherwood Rise tunnels right off the platform end. Emerging from the latter at 24½mph No 34006 accelerated to 33mph before a level mile took speed up to 48. The engine maintained this up the following climb until observation of a relaying check to 20mph at Hucknall. Then came an exceptional acceleration, to no less than 50mph on the ensuing 4 miles at 1 in 132 to top the rise in 19¼ minutes from Nottingham. Mining subsidence now took its toll with four severe slowings before the call at Staveley Town though Swain took only 41¾ minutes against the forty-three allowed. He also cut the twenty-minute allowance on to Sheffield Victoria, two permanent way checks notwithstanding, arriving 1¼ minutes ahead of schedule. After a ½ mile level there follows the 19-mile climb to Dunford Bridge and Woodhead tunnel. No 34006 had got to 40mph up the 5 miles at 1 in 120 from Oughty Bridge before a pwr check to 15mph through Thurgoland tunnel, and so lost ¾ minute on the twenty-five-minute booking from Sheffield to Penistone.

Things did not improve, for having reached 41mph on the 1 in 124/135 above Penistone, signals at Dunford Bridge brought the train down to walking pace. Taken with an uncharacteristically slow run through Woodhead tunnel, perhaps because the check was due to a train not too far ahead, and another pwr at Valehouse, Bude came into the stop at Guide Bridge all but five minutes late. Timekeeping matters weren't helped by the train having to be drawn up at both Penistone and Guide Bridge but even with a final engineering check at Fairfield, Bude was only four minutes late into Manchester (London Road).

Incidentally, on an earlier down trip the drop grate on Bude fell into the ashpan between Rugby and Leicester and could not be repositioned unless much of the fire were drawn. Being in no fit state to continue, an ex-GC class O4 2-8-0 was commandeered to haul Bude and its train to Leicester, where the problem could be resolved over a pit. Bert Hooker relates that with much of the fire removed the bars went straight back into the proper position. However, arrangements then had to be made for the engine to run 'light' to Gorton, not merely finding a path but a pilot driver to accompany the crew. As he relates '... we did not arrive in Gorton loco until about 6.30 in the evening and as usual in Manchester it was raining'. He also makes the point the hostel there wasn't a patch on the one at Upperby! The whole drop grate operating assembly was later redesigned and made more robust.

The return of Bude on 9 June was made with a train of 390 tons gross. The start is a difficult one, for the climb of 19 miles to the east end of Woodhead tunnel begins almost off the Manchester platform end. In addition, the train had to call at Guide Bridge 5 miles up the bank, the scheduled time of nine minutes appearing very demanding, particularly with a 'cold' engine. Moreover, a pwr imposed after Fairfield prevented any sort of recovery before the stop. Swain had got Bude up to 41½mph at Gorton where, it appeared, most of the works staff had turned out to see the 'stranger' pass by. Having observed the pwr at 23mph, Swain exceeded the allowance to Guide Bridge by almost 1¾ minutes. The Hall was but seconds behind though as it took ½ minute less in from Fairfield, the suggestion being driver Russell perhaps showed a little less regard for the restriction. The Hall made the better start from here and was through Mottram

This time an up (southbound) working is seen, No 34006 passing Harrow-on-the-Hill with the express from Manchester. *C. R. L. Coles*

On an unreported date and at an unreported location (likely St Pancras or Manchester London Road), No 34006 awaits with the dynamometer car attached ready for its next trial. In all cases, the attachment of the dynamometer car to the engine tender would have been undertaken at the depot at which the engine was serviced. This in itself was an involved procedure, with a number of cables requiring attachment to what were temporary fitments on the locomotive. Although not mentioned, it is likely that whenever possible the test engine was turned ready for its next duty using a triangle if one were available nearby.

(4.8 miles) a minute up on *Bude*. But the rapid acceleration that followed saw the West Country on time at Valehouse before being slowed by another pwr, to 27mph. As the Hall did not have to observe that restriction Russell was a minute ahead at Torside Crossing (10.3m). But then Swain poured on the power, sustaining 38mph up the 5 miles at 1 in 117 past Crowden and entering Woodhead tunnel at 37½mph, now 1½ minutes up on schedule and only a few seconds behind the Hall.

Although the gradient through the tunnel is at 1 in 201 *Bude* dropped back to 32½mph. Bert Hooker remarks that the tunnel was very wet and the engine was prone to the odd bout of slipping; not surprisingly then that they lost ½ minute on the five-minute booking to traverse it. The Hall meanwhile, from being ahead at Woodhead, also lost ground and its lead in the tunnel, coming to rest at Penistone one minute ahead of the forty-two allowed but ½ minute behind *Bude*. The Black 5 did not do too well on getting away from Guide Bridge and though not having to observe the pwr at Valehouse was all but 1½ minutes over time at Dunford Bridge. However, fast running down to Penistone brought no 45253 in ¾ minute to the good.

Bude's very restrained running down the hill combined with the check at Thurgoland tunnel caused a two-minute late arrival at Sheffield Victoria and a further ½ minute was

dropped to Staveley Town by reason of pwr cautions at Woodhouse and Eckington. But the superb hillclimbing ability of the West Country was again demonstrated on the near-four 1 in 100 uphill miles to Springwood tunnel and the next five rather easier miles to the summit at Pilsley, in which four minutes were gained on schedule. Thereafter, pitfall slowings prevented any further gains, though *Bude* arrived at Nottingham Victoria in 2½ minutes less than the forty-three allowed from Staveley Town.

Alone of the three, No 34006 had to observe a pwr to 30mph soon after passing Arkwright Street but with a maximum of 67mph down the 1 in 176 from Barnston tunnel came into Loughborough only 2½ minutes late. Neither of the other two engines managed to keep the sixteen-minute timing and *Bude* alone maintained it over the two brisk snippets to Leicester and Rugby. The latter was achieved by an excellent climb up the 7¼ miles at 1 in 176 through Ashby Magna, where speed had fallen only to 50mph over the 4½ miles from Whetstone, near the foot of the bank, passed at 61mph. A pwr and signal check to 5mph conspired to lose No 34006 two minutes on to Woodford, though the tight fourteen-minute timing to Brackley was bettered by 1¾ minutes and Aylesbury reached another ½ minute to the good.

No 34004 Yeovil leaving Euston at the head of an unidentified Royal Scot en route for Perth and the start of trials of the Southern engine over the Highland route.

Other than its immediate approaches and easier gradients through Stoke Mandeville and Wendover stations, the 6½ miles from Aylesbury to Dutchlands summit are almost entirely at 1 in 117. Allen describes *Bude*'s climb as '… one of the most startling exhibitions that I recorded during the whole series of tests and one to which I know of no parallel with any ex-LNER locomotive similarly loaded'. This time he was right! Perhaps the incentive was provided by Swain having to 'set back'. On the 1¼ miles to Stoke Mandeville speed had risen to 37½mph and had increased to 48mph before Wendover. The brief 1 in 264 through the station saw it rise to 50mph, '… with 395 tons of train (the passenger complement had increased considerably'), and finally to 51mph at the summit. Despite an annoying pwr on the descent at Great Missenden the Pacific cut 4½ minutes off the thirty-two-minute allowance to Rickmansworth. But the operating thereafter went awry with a prolonged signal stop before Harrow to add to the pwr there, costing some seven minutes in running. Eventually *Bude* arrived at Marylebone four minutes late, a disappointing end to what had been a very spirited trip. Allen makes no attempt to calculate the net time from Aylesbury but I would put it at no more than 50½ minutes against the fifty-seven scheduled. Of all the tests in which the light Pacifics were involved this is, I think, the most notable in revealing the true extent of their power and ability in the right hands.

That brings us then to the final route and a trip of 450 miles to reach the starting point at Perth. This was made in two stages, No 34004 double-heading a Royal Scot on the 5.05pm Euston–Holyhead train as far as Crewe and the next day double-heading another Scot on the 8.55am Crewe to Perth as far as Carlisle. There it became the train engine with a Black 5 piloting for the rest of the journey. One comment made by the pilotman north of Carlisle caused Bert Hooker some amusement. With 34004 running at 70+mph on the descent from Beattock, 'riding as beautifully as only a "West Country" could and the "Black 5" in front of us fairly leaping about', the man commented '… in all seriousness, "If he's going too fast for you, put the brake on a little bit." Apparently the irony in Swain's laconic reply, 'We can stand it if he can,' was lost on him.

The first 'learning' trip to Inverness took place with the 4.0pm from Perth on Monday, 5 July. Allen makes a comment in his record of events that bears repeating. Much of this route is single track with some quite severe curvature and, of course, passing loops with tablet catchers, another skill to be mastered. Being Nine Elms men, the crew faced nothing like this in their everyday work. Allen contends with some justification that, despite the very good showing Swain and Hooker ultimately made, a crew from say, Exmouth Junction or one of its more outlying sub-depots in Devon and Cornwall, who regularly worked over similar routes, might have been more comfortable with it, particularly in running swiftly downhill. How much the work and the results may have differed from those actually produced it is impossible to know – but it would have been fascinating to find out! (Had these tests been conducted, say, three years later, by which time four light Pacifics had been allocated to Bath Green Park shed, a Branksome crew would no doubt have relished the challenge of the Highland Line, which differed little in substance from their own heavily graded and curvaceous route over the Mendips.)

In view of the particular difficulties the line posed, Jack Swain had naturally to be very reliant on his pilotman and that raises another point. Both the Black 5 and the B1 with which *Yeovil* was 'competing' were manned by Scottish crews and in the case of the B1 at least, accompanied by Scottish pilotmen. How easily understandable then was the necessary communication on *Yeovil's* footplate between the Highland Scot and the South Londoner, another fascinating question?

The first northbound test run that Allen tabulates came on 13 July, also with the 4.0pm, which called at almost all stations *en route*. Allen himself made no trips behind any of the engines but relied on information received from several correspondents. When compared to that of the B1 a week later, this trip illustrates how the engine was restrained downhill, sometimes excessively so, surely primarily the responsibility of the pilotman. (Perhaps like the LMR man on the way north the Scot thought these strangers from the little railway in the south unused to fast travel!) The load of 380 tons gross was lightened at Aviemore by detachment of the portion routed to Inverness *via* Forres and along the coast through Nairn: the train to be taken over Slochd then weighed about 275 tons.

The brisk start from Perth saw the twelve-minute schedule to the start of the Highland Line at Stanley Junction cut by 1½ minutes, the train already being halfway up the 7-mile climb to mp 8½, more than a mile of this being at 1 in 93. *Yeovil* went over the top at 34½mph still 1½ minutes up. But then for the tablet exchange at Murthley, Swain was brought down to 33mph against the 50 or so at which a regular crew would probably make it. By doing so he lost impetus for the 2½ miles up to Kingswood Crossing, much of it at 1 in 82. But the engine again showed the hill-climbing ability of the Bulleids with a minimum of 28mph at the top and now with three minutes in hand. However, a slow approach and a stand of 2¼ minutes outside Dunkeld, while a ballast train got itself into the up loop, saw all that time lost. Another relatively slow passage of the loop at Dalguise and a pwr to 20mph soon after conspired to

bring No 34004 into the call at Ballinluig 1¼ minutes late. Another 1¾ minutes were lost on the eight minutes allowed to Pitlochry and a further minute to Blair Athol. Maybe these together put Swain on his mettle for the 17 steep uphill miles to Druimuachdar summit, mostly at 1 in 70.

As usual, assistance was provided 'up the hill', but for some reason No 14501, a Pickersgill class 3P 4-4-0 and yet to be renumbered by BR, banked *Yeovil* rather than piloted as was apparently customary. The two cut the nine-minute allowance to Struan by 1¾ minutes and then the West Country gave a startling illustration of power over the next 11¼ miles to Dalnaspidal. Instead of the thirty-one minutes scheduled, the two engines came to a stand in 19min 23sec, a start-to-stop average of all but 35mph. Whether the ancient at the back actually had been winded by the speed of ascent is true or myth is of no consequence. The fact is this was no less than 5¾ minutes faster in running time from Blair Athol than taken by the 5, which, on its runs, did not call at Struan.

Once over the summit, in just under five minutes for the 2.1 miles from Dalnaspidal, time was lost consistently by cautious progress downhill and particularly at passing loops. The three-minute excess over time for the 7¾ miles to Dalwhinnie could not be solely attributed to the 20mph slack before the station, and the slowings for tablet exchange at Inchlea and Etteridge would account for the 1¼ minutes lost to Newtonmore. (The 5 at these points was travelling at 50 and 47mph against *Yeovil's* 36mph and 33.) Further losses, of ¾ minute to Kingussie, ½ minute to Kincraig and a full minute thence to Aviemore, were due to rather slow acceleration away from the stations, possibly due to the weather. This had been bad since leaving Perth but now worsened into a typical Highland storm with very heavy rain and a strong wind. Yet in these conditions, Swain, with a train now of 275 tons only, apparently had little difficulty regaining his losses during the climb to Slochd. A pwr after Aviemore was strictly observed and Swain had got No 34004 to 45mph up the initial burst at 1 in 150, falling back only to 41mph after 1½ miles at 1 in 75 to mp88, thus recouping 1¼ minutes on the thirteen-minute booking to Carr Bridge. Fourteen minutes are allowed for the almost 5½ miles thence to Slochd, graded at 1 in 60/70 with a short intermission at 1 in 92. Swain cut two minutes off this time and retained that advantage down the winding 1 in 60 to the call at Tomatin. No less than 3½ minutes was gained on the twenty-minute schedule to Culloden Moor though mainly because neither of the conditional stops, at Moy and Daviot, was called. There followed the one and only time a mile a minute was recorded on this trip before a signal check at Milburn Junction. But arrival at Inverness was still ¾ minute less than allowed.

Allen estimates the net gain on schedule by *Yeovil* and her crew to be 20½ minutes, 'a first class performance'. But he also cites another run made on 7 July, during the familiarisation week, when No 34004 was saddled with a thirteen-coach train of some 415 tons gross for the first 23½ miles to Ballinluig. The start was slower than on the test trip and though on this occasion the tablet change at Murthly was achieved at 53mph, the various engineering slacks were as bad. Nevertheless,

Swain cut ½ minute off the forty-one-minute allowance. From Ballinluig the load was reduced to 380 tons by loss of the Aberfeldy coach but two minutes were lost to Blair Athol. No 14501 again provided assistance up the hill, though on this occasion the train took a minute more to Struan than on the breathless run with the test train, and five minutes more onward to Dalnaspidal. However, that still aggregated to seven minutes less than schedule. Point-to-point times were kept to Aviemore and, with only 165 tons to be taken on to Inverness, six minutes were gained to Slochd, where the 41mph speed had to be reduced to 30 for the loop, resulting in a net gain of fourteen minutes to Inverness.

One factor Bert Hooker mentions is leakage from the oil sump, specifically from small cracks in the casing. The opinion of Inspector Knight is that the engine '… doesn't like these sharp curves'. The problem was evidently solved, temporarily, by pressing soap into the cracks. Yet I wonder, the coupled wheelbase of a WC is 3in less than that of the Black Fives that regularly worked the route, and 18in less than that of the B1. The engine's chassis would therefore theoretically suffer less stress than either of the others in trying to straighten out those curves and particularly as the layout of the frames over the axleboxes ought to have provided less distorting leverage. That being so I'd surmise it was not so much the fault of the engine *per se* but specifically that of the sump. The power for the engine's flood lubrication system is based in this casing, the pumps being driven off the valve gear's three-throw crankshaft and delivering oil through a piped system to all points in the oil bath needing it. Did the light Pacifics working on other routes noted for curvature, those of the further-flung parts of the 'Withered Arm' for example, or later on the Somerset & Dorset, suffer from similar leakage problems? Depositing oil on the track or within the boiler cladding occasionally leading to fire was not unknown. (See Peter Smith's 'Mendips Engineman' for an example.) So, were cracks in the sump or oil bath casing cause for the one and perhaps a contributor toward the other? If so it appears to be little recorded. Whatever the case, *Yeovil* certainly suffered a small degree of leakage during her Highland stay though the soap seems to have much reduced it. *(Dare we say a 'clean record'? – Ed)*

Returning to the records again, the start from Inverness with a 'cold' engine can be a real trial. Following a level mile, the line climbs for the next 21¾ miles from sea level to 1,315ft at Slochd summit. Other than ¾ mile down through Culloden Moor the gradient is 1 in 60 for almost 3 miles, 1 in 70 for the next 3 miles and, after a slight easing through Daviot station, another 1¾ miles at 1 in 60 to mp 105¼ between Daviot and Moy. A downhill breather at 1 in 200 precedes 6 miles of relatively easy gradients to Tomatin, where the 1 in 60 resumes for the final 3½ miles to the summit. The gradient averages 1 in 87.3 for those 21¾ miles. Not only did *Yeovil* have to contend with weather conditions similar to those of the previous day but a fish train that preceded it had managed to leave a trail of unwanted lubrication on the track. Nevertheless, on the 8.20am to Perth the following morning Swain had got his engine and its 260-ton train up to 27mph on the first length of

1 in 60, increasing to 33½ on the following 1 in 70. The conditional stop at Culloden Moor was not called, enabling No 34004 to reach 50mph in the dip before climbing resumed. Having attained 28mph, *Yeovil* was already 6¾ minutes early passing Daviot and was thus eased for the rest of the climb, though making 41mph in the dip before Moy and arriving at Tomatin 5¼ minutes early. Swain made a fine getaway from this stop, covering the 3½ miles to Slochd in a ¼ minute less than schedule at no less than 37½mph. He attained no more than 56mph on the equally steep fall to Carrbridge but still arrived 2¾ minutes under the seventeen allowed. However, the nine minutes to Aviemore was exceeded by 2½ minutes due to the pwr in the approaches.

With the load now made up to twelve coaches of 375 tons gross, *Yeovil* kept time to the calls at Kingussie and Newtonmore, and then cut the eighteen minute allowance to the stop at Dalwhinnie, up the first 10¼ miles of the climb to Druimuachdar, by two minutes. Most of the rest of the route to the summit is at 1 in 80, No 34004 completing it in 10½ minutes, reaching 47½ mph on the slightly easier grades north of Balsporran and topping the climb at 44mph. With speed reduced to 41mph at Dalnaspidal to take up the single line tablet, and despite easy running thereafter, the engine was still 4½ minutes under schedule into Blair Athol. The B1 by comparison had kept none of the intermediate times, managed just 26mph at Druimuachdar and despite posting a speed of 61mph at Dalanraoch shaved just ¼ minute off the thirty-five allowed from Dalwhinnie.

No 34004 again kept time to the second to Pitlochry and despite another pwr to 26mph at Guay made an untroubled and unhurried run into Perth – other than a spot of *joie de vivre* once south of Stanley Junction by reaching 70mph at Luncarty – cutting another 4¾ minutes off the schedule. Allen estimates the net gain at twenty-one minutes.

The success of the West Country over the Highland Line later led to suggestions a number should be posted north to work it. Once 'the dust settled', reason dictated nothing came of this mainly because, being so far away from 'home' any problems arising from the unique Bulleid features might have been difficult to solve. As it was, Black Fives continued to hold sway until the end of steam in the Highlands, though double-heading of loads in excess of 260 to 280 tons – depending on the weather? – had to be resorted to.

The first part of *Yeovil*'s return trip to London proved interesting and involved double-heading the 'Day Perth'. This was a load of seventeen bogies but with an apparent shortage of engines the crew was asked if they'd be prepared to work the train on their own. Having agreed to, at the last moment signals were put back to 'danger' and a very shabby Black 5 was coupled ahead for the initial phase, to Stirling. No 34004 then took the train on to Carlisle alone, where a Scot, which would work the service through to Euston, coupled up 'inside' as *Yeovil* was due to come off at Crewe. The next day No 34004 was booked to double-head the Aberdeen Night Sleeper to Euston, due away from Crewe at 3.0am though that train ran in ninety minutes late. This had repercussions at Euston as,

A Duchess on the Southern. No 46236 City of Bradford leaving Waterloo, and from the look of it without a dynamometer car, meaning that, once again, this was a pre-trial run. The engine is a former 'streamliner', hence the sloping smokebox top and small front cab window. Both were later changed in future years. Note the engine is attached to a Riddles eight-wheel tender, the reason for which was the need to carry sufficient water. At this point it may be appropriate to add that Eric Youldon was recently in touch over the likely use of redundant members of the class to replace several at the time (1963) run-down members of the Merchant Navy type. This would have allowed the MNs to be withdrawn and replaced with engines considered to be in better mechanical condition. Unfortunately the idea was not proceeded with due to clearance issues on the up Bournemouth line at Battledown Flyover and also within Southampton Tunnel. A similar story had been recounted by former Inspector Mark Abbott and was included in an early issue of SW, both Eric and Mark commenting that the Duchess engines would have been fitted with the same type of Riddles tender as seen here. Topical.

because of the lateness, *Yeovil* was detached off the train at Willesden to make a direct journey to Nine Elms. Unbeknown to the crew, a small reception committee had convened at the terminus to welcome them back.

So then on to the *dessert*, or it may be the aroma given off by a particularly ripe *fromage*. What sort of useful data did these six months of testing produce? In summing up, Allen makes one blunt statement, that to a passenger the first priority in the operation of passenger trains – other than safety of course – is to run as implied in the timetable, to provide 'exactly what it says on the tin'. In that light he makes no apology for looking favourably on crews who made timekeeping their main objective. With some dismay, not to say exasperation, he reiterates the lack of a common standard of driving, citing in particular the extraordinary variation between the two drivers from the LMR, Byford with the Duchess and Brooker on the Scot. Why were the standards produced by these two men from the same depot poles apart,

the one consistently failing to make up lost time, the other achieving something quite out of the ordinary?

As with driving, so with conducting. As already stated, the Southern provided just two pilotmen, which brought about a consistency quite lacking in other Regions. He is also adamant that the performances put up by Southern engines 'behind which it was a joy to travel', was the most uniform. CJA also cites some exceptional power outputs on the part of the Bulleids – and, indeed, with the Royal Scot – such as that magnificent southbound assault on Shap by *Belgian Marine*, and the work by the light Pacific on the ex-GCR route. If nothing else, these confirm the tremendous steaming capability of the Bulleid boiler. One point noted with approval by E. S. Cox in his writings concerned the small drop in pressure between boiler and valve chest with a fully open regulator on the few occasions that actually occurred. (Equally, he disapproves of the majority of the work being done with part-open regulator, and not just by the Southern engines.)

There was a downside, of course. Even before the test results were published, anecdotal evidence suggested the Bulleids were rather heavier on coal and water than others on trial. Bert Hooker himself confirms the point, though at no time does he feel the fire gets away from him, that keeping it fed is unduly arduous. As he states on several occasions, he preferred to fire carefully placed half-shovels-full rather than scatter full ones. But then such heavy consumption must be set against the exceptional power outputs in such feats as outlined above. Also on the debit side were reports of much black smoke at times of coasting or running under light steam, an indication a proportion of the fuel went straight up the chimney unburned. Had the engines been using soft and fireable Kent coal that would not have surprised, but the hard Yorkshire coals fired throughout the tests, though obviously leaving some dust behind when being broken up, should not have produced an excessive display of smoke even with the engine working really hard, though that also occurred and especially on the Highland Line. Was the fact the Bulleids were not fitted with dampers a contributory factor here?

At the time Allen published his first book, the test results had not been publicised and it was not until 1950 that his slim follow-up appeared with these details summarised and discussed. The first surprise he notes is the lack of detailed information displayed in the report for each trip. For example, there is nothing about speeds attained and no point-to-point timings beyond the total sum for the journey, including stops. Signal checks and temporary speed restrictions were noted but there is nothing about the estimated time cost of these checks, which, of course, can vary from a dead stand to, say, 40mph.

CJA cites in particular the journey of *Belgian Marine* when it trialed the desultory special train from Crewe to Leighton Buzzard. The engine is shown as having lost twenty-seven minutes in running and to have experienced eighteen checks and two unbooked stops. Not one estimate appears in the record of how much time these cost or, worse, is any reason for the poor running noted that is down to the seeming incompetence or lack of initiative of the LMR operators rather than, as implied, that of the offending engine and its crew. Allen's record shows twenty-seven checks, three of them between 2 and 5mph, a stop on Camden Bank of such duration as to cause the train to take 11½ minutes over the last mile into the terminus, and several other long stretches taken at a crawl approaching a signal at 'danger'. One telling feature of this dreadful journey is that the weight of coal consumed went up from 3.61lb per drawbar-horsepower-hour when working the same train two days previously, to 3.86lb. Yet nothing in the accompanying statistics indicates why. Were the LMR motive power group at work here again?

The second strong point in this regard is the lack of any point-to-point timings. Why? That tells most strongly against crews who attempted to run to the working timetable so far as was possible but covered the sins of those that didn't. In that respect Byford on the Duchess was a particular winner, for he had a habit of dropping time uphill but on those occasions he attempted to gain it back, not always successfully, resorted to running freely – sometimes too freely – downhill. Had the crews been given instructions to run as closely to intermediate times as they could, and particularly making up lost time, and had the cost of delays in running as well as recording of the

No 46236 passing Vauxhall near the end of its journey up to Waterloo at the head of the Atlantic Coast Express – again a pre-trial run. Was it political that the train headboard was not carried? *P. Ransome-Wallis*

Another up working of the 'ACE', this time with the LMS Pacific recorded at Salisbury. A trial run on 25 June 1948. *A. F. Cook*

actual passing times at intermediate timing points been made, the overall results would surely have provided a truer reflection of performance and therefore been of some value.

The third and a most surprising omission from the official report is the estimated weight of passengers and luggage. It seems utterly beyond comprehension that tare weights were calculated so meticulously, down to two decimal places of tonnage at times, yet no attention is paid to train complements. It is as though the dynamometer car staff simply couldn't be bothered to get out of their seats and do a headcount, or take a glimpse at the volume of luggage on racks and in vans, even if it were only a simple estimate. Almost every run of the Atlantic Coast Express for example, irrespective of motive power, as well the Leeds–Kings Cross train of *Queen's Westminster Rifleman* were so full the load must have added 10 per cent or more to the tare weight. If the 'amateur' timers could calculate a reasonable figure for the gross weight of the train it was surely within the capability of the professionals conducting the trials to do so.

These seem to me to be serious omissions in a trial supposedly needed to decide the future design and construction of British Railways steam engines and, frankly, lends weight to the argument that, at base, the future had already been decided. Further, it appears to me the dynamometer car staff really had very little idea of exactly what was required of them, as though

they had never received a full and comprehensive brief. Were they working to orders or, worse, was it plain incompetence when it came to knowing how a railway is or should be run, inconceivable surely? This is not to say everything done served no purpose at all but the results would have been more meaningful, and the statistics have provided information more reflective of engines in everyday service if a little more thought had been given to the basis of performance on which the data were gathered and measured. It is common knowledge now that the Bulleids did not come out too well from these tests. But I reiterate my view that alone of the crews involved, with the exception of the LMR's Brooker who matched them, the Southern men were the only ones to whom timekeeping was a principal objective and especially in attempting to regain time lost.

So far as coal consumption is concerned the MN and WC came bottom in the league table, *French Line CGT* being the exception in one instance. While consuming 48.02lb of coal per mile on the Western Region tests, (the King ate slightly more) No 35019's per db-hp-hr output was 3.61lb, better than either the King or the Scot. MN coal consumption throughout the tests worked out at 3.60lb per db-hp-hr. But the variations between best and worst on each Region were quite small and I would suggest the consumption quite in keeping with regard to the work done.

A final view of No 46236, this time having arrived at Waterloo and in the process of leaving the terminus, ready to reverse back to Nine Elms. *P. Ransome-Wallis*

The same applies to the light Pacifics. If one takes the work on the London Midland Region for example, No 34005 is deemed to be using 5lb of coal per mile more than the 5MT, yet the coal fired per db-hp-hr is only 0.09lb more. Overall, however, these engines fared badly, using no less than 4.11lb of coal per db-hp-hr compared with 3.57lb by the B1 and 3.94lb by the Hall.

In the record of coal consumed per lb of water evaporated however, the Bulleid boiler showed its worth. The MN used 1lb of coal to steam 8.45lb of water, second only to the Duchess, and the WC managed to get 7.94lb of water steamed per pound of coal. But both classes fared badly when relating the water consumption to the output, again coming at the bottom of the list. The MN used 30.43lb per db-hp-hr while the WC needed 32.64lb. This lends much weight to the theory that weakness in the valve events of the engines meant, in general, the steam produced was not being used as efficiently as it might have been thanks, probably, to running with part-open regulator and generous cut-off position. It is pointless, if fascinating, to wonder how much improvement would have been made on these figures had Bulleid been able to install poppet valves and rotary gear as he originally intended, the necessary material being unavailable in wartime. The very short cut-offs at which the rejuvenated *Duke of Gloucester* is now capable of running ought to give a clue.

Happily there were positives. The report noted the exceptionally free-steaming boiler, with the firemen having little trouble maintaining pressure even with the engine

working hard, and the minimal drop between boiler and valve chest pressures with the regulator well open. The free-running and steadiness in riding were also noted, as was the level of output gained and sustained when required. But maybe the most satisfying from the point of view of those taking part – and here we have to thank Bert Hooker again – was the almost universal and enthusiastic appreciation of the crews who piloted Southern men on 'foreign' soil. That is proof, if proof were needed, a Bulleid 'Pacific' was an engineman's engine, if not that of the pen pushers and unimaginative accountants – and consistency is the last resort of the unimaginative. However, from conversations with enginemen who knew them the general opinion seems to be that the rebuilding carried out from 1956 removed the 'sparkle' that marked out the engines as special. Perhaps they were right, for after controlled tests made with the rebuilt No 35020 *Bibby Line,* it was concluded 'the engine gave one of the most predictable performances of all the locomotives that had been tested under the auspices of British Railways'.

Power outputs place the engines highly. No 35017, for example, registered a pull of 4.1 tons on the drawbar, or 1,260 drawbar horsepower on the climb from Corby Glen to Stoke on 25 May, (equivalent drawbar horsepower of 1,501**.) This was achieved at a speed of 51½mph with 25 per cent cut-off and 185psi showing in the steam chest. Coming up to London three days later, the near-record climb from Grantham to Stoke saw the pull at 5.19 tons and the actual drawbar horsepower reach 1,411 (equivalent dhp 1,659). This again was at 25 per cent cut-off but with 200lb in the steam chest. These figures were surpassed only by the Duchess when lifting its train up the 1 in 100 from Wakefield towards Ardsley. (*Belgian Marine* was exerting a pull of 6.14 tons, almost the same as the LMR engine, but at a slower pace that showed in the lower horsepower figures.) CJA also makes the point that the magnificent southbound climb to Shap he timed from the train on 14 May had been virtually duplicated by Jack Swain two days previously, an equivalent dhp figure of 1,920 being registered then compared with 1,929 on his run. The cut-off for these ascents was apparently 33 per cent with 215–225psi of steam in the valve chests. Outputs at these levels were also recorded northbound: no other engine came close to them.

For their size the West Countrys performed very well too, *Bude* registering the highest output of any engine on Wellington bank – express ones included – and more than holding its own over Rattery and Dainton. No 34006 also excelled on the ex-GCR route, and as noted, there set the highest recorded equivalent dhp figure in all the tests at 2,010. In this case, with the cut-off at 27 per cent and the regulator nearly full open, pressure in the steam chest was only 20psi less than the 260 in the boiler in making a speed of 67.8mph up the 1 in 176 between Whetstone and Ashby Magna. (The Duchess once registered 2,400dhp on the climb to Honiton tunnel, though it was deemed transitory whereas *Bude*'s was sustained.) Little needs to be said about *Yeovil*'s Highland exploits beyond stating her power outputs at all stages recorded left the 5 and the B1 far behind.

A final point on the tests concerned adhesion factors and the extent that slipping affected results. Both Bulleid designs had a bad reputation for picking up their wheels but were so ably handled that bouts of slipping on starting were far less than reportedly appeared normal in everyday service. Both have low adhesion factors, the West Country just on 'the right side' of the supposed optimum of 4.0 at 4.06, the MN much on the wrong side at 3.76. It is worth noting however, that both the engines notionally more powerful than the MN, the Duchess and the King, have factors of 3.75 and the latter in particular is noted for its surefootedness. On Rattery in the down direction, for example, No 35019 was slipping continuously for 2¼ miles. But with sand applied the drawbar pull rose from a maximum of 6.83 tons to 7.44 tons. However, Allen calls into question some of such recordings based on an extraordinary statement in the report concerning the Duchess. On 19 May *City of Bradford* is recorded as slipping almost to a standstill on Dainton. But Allen and another timer were aboard the train that day and though the engine did slip badly on passing Dainton box, the minimum there was 18mph, hardly a case of 'almost a standstill'. One is left to wonder if the professional and amateur recorders were actually on the same train!

One aspect of the largest 'standard' designs went very much against past practice. All five classes in the Express Passenger segment of the trials were multi-cylindered. Yet there was only one multi-cylindered 'standard' engine produced and that an afterthought to fill the gap left by the destruction of the LMS

rebuilt 'Turbomotive' No 46202 at Harrow & Wealdstone on 8 October 1952. As a 'one-off', still incomplete when the decision was made by BR to go for diesel power, a major and particular flaw in 71000 was never eliminated. Coal consumption proved very heavy, in part because of the tendency of the firebed to deteriorate and fragment due to vibration but mainly because, as a saving in first cost, the Kylchap exhaust arrangements specified with the Caprotti valve gear was not fitted. With the ability of the engine, as shown in tests at Swindon under the eminent Sam Ell, to work with the cut-off as low as 3 per cent, need of this apparatus to clear the exhaust was essential. As E. S. Cox commented rather sadly, '... this engine could have been a world beater'. Was he being prophetic? With the skill, time and opportunity as well as, most particularly, the will of the preservationists this grand engine has now fulfilled its potential. It may be noted that, other than No 71000 and the class 9 freight engines, all the 'standard' classes were deemed 'Mixed-Traffic' – and in reality the latter should also have been.

So what did the Bulleids provide to the new standard range? To coin a phrase, 'not a lot', although one thing was the driving wheel diameter of 6ft 2in as used in the larger engines. (Neither did the GWR and LNER designs contribute much.) Cox notes that with a modern front end the ability to reach and maintain 90mph with wheels of this dimension had been decisively demonstrated by the Southern engines – but not during the trials be it said! Note, however, he does not relate this to piston speed. With a stroke of 28in that of the Britannias, the Clans, the 5MTs and the sole 8P would be rather higher at any given rate than a Bulleid with its 24in stroke. Cox also notes the work of the 7P/5F West Country class had been impressive enough to show there was scope for developing an engine of 18½-ton axle loading in this category – though 'without the poor efficiency and mechanical complexities' of the Bulleids. The outcome, the 6MT Clan class, turned out to be an engine of so little advance on the very successful class 5MT, orders subsequent to the first ten were all cancelled.

The MN also provided the three-part ashpan to the Pacific designs and the layout of the frames. In the Bulleid engines, the horn guides are welded to the frames and the frames mounted over the centre line of the axleboxes. In this way offset loading of the spring hangers is avoided. However, in the other designs, including the 9F with its wide firebox, the usual arrangement of offsetting the horn guides was resorted to because of the need to get the frames between the backs of the driving wheels and the maximum width of the narrow firebox. (The original layout for a heavy freight engine had a 2-8-2 wheel arrangement with a Britannia boiler. The trailing pony was eventually dispensed with and the coupled wheelbase went to five axles to maximise adhesion. A unique boiler design thus became necessary.) The Bulleid method of shrinking tyres to wheel rims was also adopted, there being no fixtures at all between the two. The pony truck, which gave its engine crews such a smooth ride, was also adopted for the Pacifics without change other than substituting laminated springs for coils. At the time breakage of coil springs was common, if much reduced though not entirely eliminated in later years by putting in stronger springs.

Later, and so far as the Southern was concerned, many 'standard' engines found themselves roaming the Region from Cornwall to Kent, in particular 4-6-0s of both the 73xxx and 75xxx varieties and the 4MT 2-6-0s in the 76xxx series. Class 4MT and 2MT tank engines – including incidentally the Ivatt version of the latter – also appeared in numbers though none of these classes had any specifically 'Bulleid' features. It may be noted that for some months in 1948 two LMR Fairburn 4MT 2-6-4 tank engines, Nos 42198/9, were tested over all three sections of the Southern Region independently of the main trial. As a result Brighton began to turn out members of this class for local use, and latterly started construction alongside them of an order for forty-four of the BR 'standard' class 4MT 2-6-4T engines, Nos 80010-53, to be divided between the Southern, Scottish, North Eastern and London Midland Regions. These appeared in 1951. In time all the Brighton-built Fairburns were transferred north of the Thames, mainly to Scotland, the Southern receiving 'standards' in return. (Brighton completed 130 Standard 4MT engines between 1951 and 1956.)

Britannias featured regularly on the Western and Eastern Divisions, Nos 70004 and 70014 being allocated to Nine Elms/Stewart's Lane respectively for a period in the 1950s, to 'show the flag' on the 1951 Royal Wessex, a service using new BR Mk1 coaches and a Britannia, and also further east on the Continental Boat trains. The many Bulleid Pacifics in traffic made it unnecessary to allocate more. But I wonder how many light Pacifics might have been transferred to the Great Eastern line had BB *Sir Archibald Sinclair*'s brief foray out of Liverpool Street in 1949 been followed up? Or was that engine's visit responsible for the posting of the early Britannias to Stratford and Norwich, with a revolutionary effect on the timetable? Whatever the case, Richard Hardy writes, 'How we enjoyed that machine!' (He was, of course, to have closer acquaintance with the Bulleids for almost 2½ years following his appointment as shed master at 73A (Stewart's Lane) in August 1952.)

On its final day on the GER line *Sir Archibald* was set to haul a thirteen-coach train from Norwich to London, a train that included the General Manager's saloon with the formidable Leslie Preston Parker – incidentally a great supporter of the Britannias from the design stage onward – among its passengers. All was set for a good run when, as Hardy puts it, '… we climbed the 1 in 84 to Trowse Upper as if it were 1 in 300'. But only a few miles out of Norwich the steam pipe supplying the reverser broke, meaning the engine could neither notch up nor reverse. Nothing daunted, having advised the managerial members in the saloon what had happened, the train continued its journey. But as Richard Hardy asks, what other engine could have run the 107 miles to London in full gear with 60lb or less in the steam chest and still kept time on a demanding schedule with a thirteen-coach train? (But an awful lot of coal was consumed!)

So was this the end of locomotive interchanges on the Southern? Certainly not, for as we know various 'foreign' engines ventured on to the region whether it be on through workings, 'borrowed' (usually by Eastleigh) after repairs, as replacements during crises and of course on special trains. (Not forgetting the WR pannier tanks that were a common sight at Folkestone Harbour and also on ecs workings from Waterloo.) So how about Southern engines that ventured elsewhere? Again special workings, the Bulleid Pacifics that were loaned to the Great Eastern section and on paper at least the Exmouth Junction allocation was all transferred to the Western Region in the 1960s, but a Q1 … ? Well according to the late Jeffery Spence this is a view of an unidentified Q1 near Woodford Halse on the Great Central main line in 1949 – unless, of course, YOU know different …?

Opposite: For its size it must be admitted the rebuilt Royal Scot performed well and was represented on the Southern Region by No 46154 The Hussar. The engine is seen at the head of the 16.50 Waterloo to Plymouth (which it will haul as far as Exeter Central) and again when entering Waterloo on the return duty. *E. S. B. Elcome and C. R. L. Coles*

Perhaps his words following sum up best these remarkable engines whose innovative design and characteristics were too much to bear for the cautious inhabitants of 222 Marylebone Road: 'The Bulleid Pacifics, wayward, difficult, brilliant, fascinating, had that very human trait of rising to the occasion.' And those in preservation still do. Perhaps we should finish then by raising a glass of a favourite *liqueur* in a toast to a unique engineer and his masterpieces.

*It is quite as likely the challenge was made by, or at least emanated from, the LNER Chairman, William Whitelaw, to his opposite number on the GWR, Sir Felix Pole, who was never afraid to fight in defence of his company.

**Horsepower is the rate at which work is done, 1 hp being 550 foot-pounds per second. (I have no idea how to translate that into non-imperial speak!) Drawbar Horsepower is the actual hp exerted by the engine between tender and train at specific points, being a measure of the power required to overcome the resistance of the train to motion and, where climbing, the downward pull of gravity. In locomotive tests drawbar hp figures relate to output on level track and calculations using well known and proven formulae have thus to be made to add to those figures the additional power necessary for the engine to move itself and its tender and train against the pull of gravity. The total figure is then expressed as 'Equivalent Drawbar Horsepower'.

Bibliography

The Locomotive Exchanges, Cecil J. Allen, Ian Allan Ltd., 1949.

New Light on the Locomotive Exchanges, Cecil J. Allen Ltd., 1950.

Nine Elms Engineman, A. E. 'Bert' Hooker, Bradford Barton. (Undated).

Bert Hooker, Legendary Engineman. A. E. Hooker, Oxford Publishing Company, 1994.

Two Million Miles of Train Travel, Cecil J. Allen, Ian Allan Ltd., 1965.

Bulleid, Last Giant of Steam, Sean Day-Lewis, George Allen & Unwin, 1964.

British Railways Standard Steam Locomotives, E. S. Cox, Ian Allan Ltd., 1966.

British Pacific Locomotives, Cecil J. Allen, Ian Allan Ltd., 1962.

Locomotives Illustrated No 7, 'King Arthurs', Derek Cross, Ian Allan Ltd., 1976.

Locomotives Illustrated No 12, Bulleid Merchant Navies, Derek Cross, Ian Allan Ltd., 1977.

Locomotives Illustrated No 28, Bulleid Light Pacifics, Derek Cross, Ian Allan Ltd, 1982.

Loco Profile: Royal Scots, Profile Publications Ltd., 1971.

Steam in the Blood, R. H. N. Hardy, Ian Allan Ltd., 1971.

Railways in the Blood, R. H. N. Hardy, Ian Allan Ltd., 1985.

Steam was my Calling, E. S. Beavor, Ian Allan Ltd., 1974.

Mendips Engineman, P. W. Smith, Oxford Publishing Company, 1972.

Southern Region Steam Album, S. C. Nash, Ian Allan Ltd., 1974.

The Changing Southern Scene 1948–1981, Michael Baker, Ian Allan Ltd., 1981.

The Somerset & Dorset in the Fifties, Vol 1, 1950–1954, Ivo Peters, Oxford Publishing Company, 1980.

Red for Danger, L. T. C. Rolt, 3rd ed., David & Charles, 1976.

British Railways Pre-Grouping Atlas and Gazetteer, Ian Allan Ltd.,

Track Atlas of Great Britain, TRACKmaps, 2009.

Gradient of the British Rail Line Railways, Ian Allan Ltd, 2016.

Various editions of Ian Allan Ltd ABCs, 1942 onwards.

The Lost Archives of Stephen Townroe
Part 3

Continuing on with this remarkable collection we restart at 1938 with a brief look at Royal Ascot 1938, held from 14–17 June.

The special trains operated in addition to the normal service meant a ground plan was needed to ensure stock was berthed as necessary and certainly as rapidly as possible. Here a shunt move is being authorised by a ground signalman using a green flag – his red flag (darker in colour when seen next to his trousers) is ready for use. Although not confirmed, it would appear trains are being stabled on the down line, the man authorising movement in this area. Ascot 'A' box is just out of camera on the left.

We assume checking the locomotive workings … Mr E. S. Moore, the Western Division Locomotive Superintendent, seemingly deep in thought at Ascot.

Someone who is definitely not wondering where his engines and crews are is this man. We can be certain his paper is certainly dealing with different placings!

Opposite and left: SCT's records indicate this pair of views were taken around late autumn 1938 and depict a test of new lifting gear for the 'new Portmouth Electric Trains'. The location is believed to be Fratton with most of the attention centred upon the method of keeping the sling from damaging the bogie, shoe beams, and bodysides. This would prove to have been a very useful exercise just a short time later in the Second World War, although it must also be said that the occasions were fortunately rare when (in normal service) it was necessary to lift a unit because of an incident.

Up to now it would appear SCT's role at this time was almost a roving commission, attending various incidents – not always when things had gone wrong. Here he has recorded one of the SR diesel-electric shunters at Hither Green with particular reference to the sanding gear and what appears to be an excessively worn brake-block and, perhaps most interesting of all, a glimpse at part of the driver's cab.

This small series is undated but recorded in his index as 'Replacing Ford Bridge, Sussex, prior to electrification' – which took place from 3 July 1938. The original bridge consisted of five spans over the (tidal at this point) River Arun, the middle one having a minimum 41ft clearance for vessels. The original centre section could be opened (by hand!) by drawing the girders back over wheels through chain and wheel gearing. Already the conductor rails are in place ready for July, whilst in the background is an excellent example of an LBSCR 'signal bridge'.

Inspector Jack Watson and 'Schools' No 930 'Radley' leaving Waterloo on what was reported to be a special train for 'brake tests'. The headcode indicates the destination was Southampton. Unfortunately no other details are given.

The 'Green Train', meaning the 'Bournemouth Limited' (although it also served destinations between Bournemouth and Weymouth) running at more than 70mph near West Stafford, approximately 2 miles east of Dorchester. This was likely taken soon after SCT's first management position in charge at Dorchester depot.

In his own words SCT recounted, 'It was really only interest and not the salary that kept me working for the railway,' the former certainly proven with his photographic legacy. Here we have the best of what was a small series of views taken showing a shunt move taking place at Dorchester – unfortunately all taken into the afternoon sun.

The Southern Way   Issue 38

Shortly after taking charge at Dorchester we have a record of a fire that destroyed a hut on the depot site. SCT does not give the reason – but did stop to take several views of the burning building. The tarred sleepers on the outside would have added to the conflagration. I particularly like the view of the man using his extinguisher on the depot coal stack, fortunately as it transpired with success in preventing this from catching light.

Opposite and overleaf: To conclude this issue's instalment, we have two views on the main line near Templecombe. The first from ground level is of T9 No 117 piloting a King Arthur. The second is from the landing stage of the adjacent water tower (rank hath its privileges!) and this time with King Arthur No 789 on a down working. No dates are given although it is likely both were taken around the time SCT moved to take charge at Yeovil in April 1938 and just six months after having been appointed to Dorchester.

48

Rebuilt
The Letters and Comments Pages

We start this issue's notes with a veritable feast from Neil Knowldon, (Hon. Membership Secretary of the Southern Railways Group: membersec@srg.org.uk)

'Kevin, Apologies for the delay in commenting on *SW36* but I've only just got my copy … anyway, thanks for including some of my comments in 'Rebuilt' – Eric Youldon has since been kind enough to correct me on my suggestion that "plain" Light Pacific rods might have started out on "Merchant Navies" at Barry: I'd overlooked the difference in rear coupled wheelbase, of course !

'Further to *SW35* – and my comments on (pigeon) van trains – it doesn't look like anyone's commented on other van matters of interest: on p21 there's an 'Air Control Van' between the Pull-Push set and the M7 (Not one of the wartime original conversions but one of the short-lived plywood bodied replacements); the second van in the upper picture on p30 is one of the three (by that date) former ferry brake vans; on p59, what is in tow is a 'Van B' – or just 'B' in B.R. parlance – a 'PMV' never had guard's accommodation though its function, otherwise, was much the same.

'Now to *SW36* … on p25, the vertical bars at the top – which is actually at the right-hand side (they're – er – shown horizontal) – are, in fact the eight longitudinal roof girders mentioned and the curved plate is the firebox crown forced down across the firehole: the failed stays show up clearly as black dots on the crown and the line of holes must be where the crown has been torn away from the throat plate rivets (out of shot to the right … er, that's forward).'

Yes I am aware of this. Somehow the photo got turned through 90°, whether that was me at the time of submission or subsequently I cannot be certain, but my apologies all the same.

Recent discussion on a particular internet forum mentioned the 'luggage bridges' at certain stations. Two in particular were mentioned, Eastleigh – now long swept away following the abolition of the former Platform 1, and also Brockenhurst, where the infrastructure still exists even if I understand the facility itself has not been used for some time and there is also now 'no one authorised to use it'. The single lever ground frame locked the bridge in place and prevented the signalman allowing any signalled movement into the platform. *S. W. Circle 'J. Eyers collection'*

'Now to the "Mid-Kent Railway Part 2": Elmers End: p47/48: As you can see in the picture, Elmers End station building did not straddle the tracks in Clock House/Woodside style. The "up" side building (left) was the one destroyed by fire and replaced in "Maze Hill" style brutalism – 1973 was long before Network South East days, of course … the Station Master's house – visible on the "down" side – had gone long before that. Jeremy comments on the gap in the canopy after the war – you'll see that the bombing also destroyed a single-storey extension (waiting room?), which left its scar on the house: unfortunately the 1961 canopy only replaced the surviving stretch and there's a very wet (at times) gap between it and the footbridge. Regrettably the tall brick rotary converter building only survived until 2002 and the space became yet more car park. Unfortunately, Jeremy is wrong implying that the northward platform extensions and bridge reconstruction were in connection with the introduction of 'Networker' stock: this was part of a later scheme to increase all platforms on the line to take twelve-car trains (Though with the current fleet they WOULD have to be 'Networkers' as there's no way you could make twelve out of five-car class 376s.) … unfortunately this was money wasted as no twelve-car train has ever run to my knowledge!

'Bingham Road: p50/51: It's very noticeable on the tram, approaching from either direction, that the line rises then drops suddenly to street level at the "Addiscombe" tram stop beneath where the station used to be – then rises and descends, again, on departure.

'Sanderstead: p51: In electric days, at least, Elmers End services terminated at the "down" platform then ran forward in the Oxted direction before crossing to the "up" platform for departure; I don't know whether the third rail was retained after the W.&.S.C. closed – it certainly wasn't long before it would have been wanted again for the East Grinstead scheme.

'Tramlink: p51: To put it in context, the 90° curve from the Woodside Tunnel up to Sandilands tram stop was the site of the recent fatal crash.

'Elmers End: p51: Though the curve out of Elmers End was, indeed, largely of check-railed bullhead track until very recently, both lines are now laid with flat bottom rails and the check-rail is no longer deemed necessary!

'Eden Park: p51: The 'timber' buildings are not quite what they seem – maybe ten years ago they were reclad (again in a passable S.E.R. style) in UPVC! (There is actually a small shelter on the "down" side – at the top of the subway stairs.)

'West Wickham: p53: Among the more notable clientele was no less a person than James Staats Forbes, chairman of the "rival" L.C.D.R. (!) who lived locally.'

Also one time chairman of at least one other railway, the Didcot, Newbury & Southampton Co.

'The photo on p52 shows the "up" dock siding in front of the 'box: the latter was actually in a slight recess in the cutting side. (Behind the 'box you might just be able to make out what appears to be another building. I have absolutely no idea what this was but there's a hollow in the top of the cutting side there to this day.) While suburban sprawl did bring vast traffic increases to the West Wickham and Hayes Railway – probably rather later than the promoters hoped – it's still a fairly "green" area and the bridge in the background of the photo is one of three hereabouts that were built for roads but have only ever carried footpaths.

'Hayes: p53: The final approach to Hayes from the summit at Teipigs Lane bridge (lovely name) is, as Jeremy says, on a sharp right-hand curve – BUT the boundary fence goes straight on from the bridge and I suspect there might originally have been plans to put the station closer to the village in that direction. Like many termini, I guess, there were suggestions for extensions both before and after the line was built but, obviously, nothing came to fruition.

'Rolling stock: p56: Reference to 3SUB units is misleading as this was never an official name and has sort of 'stuck' to the three-car units since the first 4Sub units (official name) appeared – they were all soon augmented to 4Sub format, of course. The original Eastern Section sets had one more compartment per coach because they were built on longer frames then the Western section sets – not by "squeezing the knees" as Bulleid did with his eleven compartment horrors later.

'Traffic 1: Jeremy was wise to avoid any mention of the current London Bridge situation: having endured a few years while Charing Cross trains didn't call there, the boot is now on the other foot and it is the Cannon Street services that will pass through non-stop until the station rebuild is completed. (The former S.E.R. offices on Tooley Street have already disappeared: see p81).

'Traffic 2: While local traffic was, seemingly, always sparse on the Woodside and South Croydon, it was often used to keep excursions, hoppers, etc, away from the main lines – especially when the Crowhurst Curve gave options into Kent.

'Traffic 3: Happily Boris's plans for sticking the Hayes Line on to the Bakerloo seem to have died a death – the thought of running a service with seven (max) 17 metre coaches into the expensively stretched twelve car platforms was just plain daft, surely! (Not to mention the chaos of trying to bring the "tube" to the surface without disrupting the established operation.)

'Bibliography: p58: A notable omission is Trevor Woodman's *The Railways to Hayes* ISBN: 0950811009 published by the Hayes Village Association for the centenary in 1982.

'Midhurst: p68: The carriage that was briefly encountered appears to be a brake from one of the S.E.C.R.'s late non-birdcage trio sets – would be interesting to know how it came to be available in or around Brighton.

'"Southern Blue": p91: No, no electric stock of Southern origin ever ran in Blue AND Grey – many Bulleid-style EPB units did, but they were all B.R. built, of course.'

The intended reference was 'Southern' in the generic sense rather than a specific 'Southern Railway', apologies for the confusion.

'… and I thought the shot of 4EPB No.5176 looked familiar (*Southern Blue*) –the unit was repainted into plain blue for its last few weeks (months?) in traffic and was used with other stock shuttling between Hastings and Robertsbridge (photo) in connection with an open day at St Leonards Depot on 10/11 September 1994. It was subsequently 'preserved' – as was 'original' unit 5001 – but currently languishes even further from Southern Suburban territory in Northamptonshire AND Warwickshire … No 5001 went to make razor blades in the end.

I was also delighted to hear from Greg Beecroft on the subject of the Southern 'glass house' signal boxes:

'Thanks for the review of Southern "glass house" signal boxes in SW36. Strood was the only place to have two boxes to this design. Like Bognor Regis, the box at Richmond has curved windows to the rear, even though there was never any track behind it. Deal also has curves to the rear, but was this standard for boxes with no ground floor extensions? Wimbledon A box, which survives as a training school, has rounded ends to the ground floor extensions. I think this is unique, unless the contemporary box at Twickenham was the same. The positioning of the signal box name was revised after the first two were built. As your photograph shows, Surbiton had individual letters applied to the brickwork just below the operating floor windows. Woking has the name on a concrete plaque centrally placed on the first floor brickwork. It has a concrete band right round the first floor, midway between floor level and the window sills, and I think this was also a unique feature. The name on others is on a plaque on the concrete band separating ground and first floors. Portsmouth Harbour has no windows at ground floor levels, but a blank expanse of brickwork, as at Strood Junction, was avoided by introducing decorative brick panels.

'Boxes to this design still in use are Deal, Richmond and Bognor Regis, though Richmond only controls the line from Gunnersbury. The closed signal box at Woking is a listed building.'

Now for one whose origins I regret I deleted – sorry – however, I suspect it is from Chris Sayers-Leavy:

'What I did not expect to uncover whilst writing this message – was a Suffragette connection with Eden Park station. Apparently (this probably needs verifying) a bomb was planted by the Suffragettes in the ladies waiting room at Eden Park station – but the clockwork mechanism stopped – and it failed to go off. It was discovered on Saturday, 14 June 1913 – ten days after Emily Wilding Davison ran out in front of the King's horse during the Derby.

'Reference the comments from Trevor Davis in the Rebuilt section on p86 – I may have a different explanation – although it is tenuous. Re the picture of the Queen Mary in Romford coal yard, in Mike King's Southern Rolling Stock in Colour publication. I joined the LM Electrification section in late 1977 at Bedford and at the time the GE 6.25kv conversion scheme was coming to an end – and all the vehicles that they had used were transferred across to Bedford. In our allocation were a number of these brake vans that were used on 'works trains'. A number of these had been used on the Weaver Junc.–Gretna

Junc. electrification – where there was a problem of working with rail cranes that did not have 'power brakes' on the gradients "across the border" and we continued to use them between Bedford and St Pancras on the "Midland Suburban Electrification" scheme. I was responsible for these vehicles – as I was the "Works Trains and Plant Inspector" – a grandiose job title for a relatively low graded job. The number of this van does not strike a chord – but from memory we had at least Nos 56298–56303 and although the picture shows 56304 apparently "in traffic" – it would have been on the cusp of being transferred to departmental use. I can vouch for their riding qualities – the best there ever was for a brake van, but the large cabin area could be a very cold and draughty space, unless you had a good fire going inside, but the days of brake vans being "coaled up" in yards had long gone by then … and although fitted with a good stove, any wood used had to be broken up into small pieces in order to get the fuel in … '

Now from Alastair Wilson:

'Here are just a couple of extra comments on Rebuilt from SW37. Firstly, relating to Jeremy Clarke's comments on the length of the Hastings DEMUs. In steam days, the maximum length of a train for Hastings, via the SER route, was eleven Maunsell Hastings-line coaches (which included a Pullman), plus a "Schools" at the head (or if something had failed somewhere, an L1).These would fit into the appropriate platform at Cannon Street (not sure if they would fit the appropriate platform (6?) at Charing Cross but I think they must have done). If the idea was to use two-six coach units, plus a separate diesel power unit for the heavy business trains (the 5.6 p.m. ex-Cannon Street was the most important, always loading to eleven coaches in steam days) then undoubtedly there would have been length problems. Had they had to double head two six-coach units, they would have been in trouble.

'As to his comments on the LNER's use of the Met's K class tanks on passenger services, that really was a last resort for the Neasden shedmaster – I used to live at Amersham in those days, and was an assiduous watcher of trains from the age of about seven onwards. It was very rare to see anything other than an A5 "Coronation" tank, though I did see several of the handsome H class 4-4-4Ts before they migrated to Nottinghamshire, and on one memorable occasion before the war, one of the G class 0-6-4Ts ("Daddy, daddy, it's got a name!!" I cried as it pulled into Amersham before taking us to Rickmansworth and electric traction). But since virtually every train stopped at all stations from Rickmansworth to Aylesbury, there wouldn't have been too much time between station stops to work up to a dangerous speed, nor did the schedule require it. But I do remember seeing one of the big lumbering Robinson 2-6-4Ts (the original LNER class L1) at the head of a passenger train on one occasion – again, no doubt, the result of a failure somewhere else on the line.

'Further on, Keith Dawes talks about his time on the Chi goods and the Wye at Chichester. There was, I think, just one other steam service terminating at Chichester at that time (the early-to-mid 1960s, I assume; before that time the motive

The short-lived Regency Belle awaiting departure from Victoria on 18 April 1964. The train name has since been resurrected on the Bluebell railway with Pullman travel.

power was usually an S15 or occasionally an H15): there was an early afternoon parcels from Portsmouth which ran into the up bay at the newly rebuilt Chichester station (we still had a regular half-hourly stopping electric service to Portsmouth Harbour – usually a 2-NOL, sometimes a 2-BIL – which usually used the two bays). The afternoon parcels was usually headed by a class 2 tank, which could scoot back to Fratton without worrying about turning.

'Then, in Jeffery Grayer's article The Hills of the South, the caption to the map of the area mentions that on the Chichester to Midhurst line, the stations were still shown, although the line "had closed four years previously". Not strictly true: it had closed to passengers in 1935 but the line and the three stations named remained open for freight until 1951 – and the southern stub to Lavant stayed open to 1965 for sugar beet traffic and even later as an extended siding from Chichester for gravel into the 1970s.

'Finally, my mind running on from "bucket lists", this is one where it's a case of what I wish I hadn't done. Query – where might one have photographed a clerestory coach in Midland lake livery, lettered "Midland", under GNR-type balanced semaphores, in a station painted in WR chocolate and cream colours, while the station name board said "Perth"? Answer – in Perth, Western Australia. I took such a photo in 1962, thinking "Scoop! The Railway Magazine will love this". But when the slide was processed, I discovered that the whole thing was so out of focus as to be totally unusable. (I had just been photographing an exotic flower in close up and had forgotten to refocus.) Talk about kicking myself!'

Now to Andrew Harris and reference carriage roof boards:

'A little anecdote you might find amusing. Many years ago during one of my visits to that Aladdin's cave that was collectors

The long-closed New Romney and Littlestone-on-Sea station on the short branch from Romney Junction – itself on the line from Appledore to Dungeness. Opened in 1884, the branch closed on 6 March 1967. The view is looking towards the actual end of the branch line a short distance beyond the level crossing. At one time operation was interesting to say the least. A train would leave Appledore conveying passengers for the terminus at New Romney (the suffix was added in 1888) but, arriving at Lydd, all the passengers for New Romney would alight. They would wait there until the train had continued to the other terminus at Dungeness and returned again to Lydd. Here the procedure would be reversed – literally – the passengers from Dungeness, the majority destined for Appledore, would themselves now alight to be replaced by the waiting New Romney group. The train would again reverse direction and venture up the branch to the New Romney destination. The name New Romney will be familiar as the terminus of the narrow gauge Romney, Hythe and Dymchurch branch, which system for many years received coal via the standard gauge siding beyond the level crossing seen. New Romney station had at one time boasted a small turntable, the site of the standard gauge railway now lost under an industrial estate. *John Bailey*

corner at Euston with my son together with a school friend we bought a full-length board. Stephen chose "Ocean liner Express Waterloo–Southampton Docks", but how to get it home? We ended up walking from Euston to Charing Cross, 4EPB to Croydon with them in the aisle, 4VEP to Redhill and finally walking to Reigate. But what I have always remembered was that at no point did any member of the public or railway staff query or make any reference to them on our journey.'

'Happy days … I am sure like many I wished I had invested in railwayana years ago. I did acquire a signal arm and spectacle plate and promptly dropped it on the foot of the conductress on the way home. Not surprisingly, she made me walk the rest of the way … Signal was 'cleared' years ago to make room for family commitments.

Now more from Chris Sayers-Leavy:

'I'm currently still digesting the content of the latest edition of *SW35* and may well write to you later on, in a more conciliatory vein, but for now, my comments relate simply to the quoted correspondence from Howard Bolton on p55/56 of your Rebuilt feature. You will recall that I also commented on the picture of the Leader firebox being dismantled that was published in your previous 'Seeing life in Black & White' feature.

'I have to say, that I feel obliged to leap to Bulleid's defence – if for no other reason other than that he is unable to do this in person, and that as such he is an easy target to pillory.

'Don't get me wrong – you will be aware that we have corresponded previously on Mr Bulleid and what he got up to – and for me personally, I am still considering the pros and cons of his achievements and failures and whilst I am currently erring in his favour; my mind is far from made up on the matter and I may well change my views as I learn/understand more about the man and his motives, etc.

'I have also commented to you previously on how academics and professional engineers can "close ranks" and ostracise "one of their own" just because they dared to "think outside the box", to use a modern phrase. The pleasure gained by some at the expense of another is very unsavoury, bordering on a "blood lust" and in my view very unprofessional. It has unfortunately become "fashionable" to "bash" Bulleid and put him down at every opportunity.

'There is no doubt that Bulleid was very much a "Marmite Man" – you either love him or hate him and there are no other intermediate categorisations or "shades of grey" in peoples' assessments. Howard Bolton stops short of actually calling Bulleid a "madman", and I am aware here that you may well have edited his full comments, but it is suggested that Bulleid was a "madman" by association and just because he dared to try

something that was not *de rigueur* within the steam engineering fraternity. In my view the "madman" tag is very unjust and unfair. Had Bulleid been a complete failure as an engineer, we would probably not even be talking about him now but, as it happens, there were a number of successful and innovative designs, albeit that he does seem to have "lost" his way in later life.

'It is still not clear to me why Bulleid settled on certain design scenarios; I agree that chain-driven valve gear and sleeve valves turned out to be "blind alleys" but we must also remember that both these concepts were being used elsewhere in the automotive and aircraft industries with varying degrees of success. I personally can't blame Bulleid for "trying" but he should have known when to give up on these ideas and that is the danger of being the top man; no one else challenges you, not, that is, if they value their future employment!

'It is well known that it is a very fine line that separates genius and madness and personally I would stop well short of using either term when discussing Bulleid and his work. He does, however, seem to have been "obsessed by proving a case" for modern steam traction, when all around him post-Second World War "engineering" had moved on and the internal combustion engine was coming to the fore (albeit at an increased cost of complexity and construction) while the SR was already championing early diesel electric traction, let alone the electrification/electric traction opportunities.

Examples from the drawing board during the time of Messrs Bulleid, Maunsell and Adams. In the first category is No 34081 92 Squadron. We also have a Q, possibly No 30532, and finally the unmistakable shape of B4 No 30096. The location is the rear of the running shed at Eastleigh. The post supported by guy-wires sprouting from what appears to be the chimney of No 30096 displayed a red light at the top as the running shed was located literally at the northern end of the perimeter of what was then referred to as Eastleigh airport. Of the engines seen, Nos 34081 and 30096 survive in preservation. *John Bailey*

'I'm afraid that the reality was that the world was rapidly changing during Bulleid's later years and he was still very much an "Edwardian mechanical engineer" in the late twentieth century, but he does not deserve to be castigated for "trying" or to be burdened with an accolade that is clearly inappropriate.'

At this stage let me say as Editor that my own views on much of Mr Bulleid's work are probably well known. I tend to regard him as a flawed genius. He was a man who, and I have used this phrase before, had a lifetime of ideas and only a short time in which to create them in practice. Time would not be kind to him. I read somewhere once that when trying to summarise Mr Bulleid we should recall that if other professionals can sometimes disagree, why should locomotive engineers not do so? Indeed, in the locomotive history of Britain's railway we already see countless examples of this, with engineers pursuing different paths but all intended to achieve similar aims.

We should also not forget that as far as the lineside enthusiast was concerned, there was a world of difference between admiring observation and having to work upon, maintain, or even design and build a particular engine. (I don't think I have ever seen anything recorded anywhere about how easy/difficult it was to erect a particular engine type comparing one with another.)

As we progress through life our favorites inevitably become more fixed, usually based upon memories of long ago. I would argue that we unintentionally compare one with another and in so doing, subconsciously create pedestals upon which to place our favorite type and a deep hole in which to discard others. Thus we conveniently ignore perhaps important aspects for the sake of personal choice. There is nothing wrong with this, I (and I suspect 99 per cent of readers) would fall into this category. Returning to Mr Bulleid, however, and notwithstanding my personal criticism of some of his works and indeed his behaviour, both of which I have learned though study, I still stick by everything I have written in the past; the man was a genius but one who also needed to be controlled. Hence my comment in my personal 'Bucket List' statement a few issues back, if I could meet him (at some point in the future) I would still like to ask just one question, 'Why?'

I should add that Chris continues with his own slant on my recent editorial in which I dealt with political correctness. Having carefully considered the likely consequences I have made the decision not to reproduce most of his comments. This is certainly not because I may personally agree or disagree but because I respect the views of others, and there would no doubt have been others who would have taken a different view. Suffice to say, as long as I remain editor I intend to adopt a non-partisan view when it comes to politics. My editorial was as much personal as it was tongue in cheek, so I close this piece of correspondence with a single note from a correspondent, 'Yes I will be greatly offended, living in Kent, if you keep going on about "West Countries"; I demand that you change your policy; to refer only to "Battle of Britains" !!!!!!!' I sit corrected.

We have received several positive comments about the Jim Seddon images in 'Counting down to July 2017' that have appeared to date and, as you will see, continue again in this issue. One reader probably sums up the words of many, 'I'm very pleased that you are running this as a feature – just as I remembered it all! I wait to see if I appear in any of the pictures … '

Well, even if you don't in this issue, do look out for more in *SW39*.

___

Now from Jeremy Clarke, who wishes to comment on Rebuilt in *SW36*:

'Hi Kevin, may I add my two-penn'orth to the comments on this engine – the Holcroft/Anderson N class conversion – in *SW36*? (I should add I have not seen the original article: none of my local outlets appears to believe SW might command local interest – more fool them!) But I can confirm Chris Sayer-Leavy's belief that Maunsell was not an experimenter. By the time he took up the reins at Ashford in 1913 he had already showed himself more of an admirable administrator with a knack of picking the right subordinates to support him. That is not to say that he did not interest himself in developments elsewhere and study anything closely that took his eye, which may perhaps explain his acceding to the syndicate's request to carry out the experiments on No A816. Then there is the question posed in the caption to the photo on p79 about the time it was taken. There is a picture of the nearside by H. C. Casserley at Eastleigh on p27 in *A Pictorial History of Maunsell Locomotives by Brian Haresnape* (Ian Allan Ltd., 1977, ISBN 0711007438.) The caption intimates that the picture was taken 'during experiments', though no precise date is given, and goes on to point out that the square chimney was later superseded by a 'more conventional one'. If so, that would tend to confirm experiments were still in progress when the p79 photo was taken. Conversion back to a true N took place in mid-1935.

'I suspect Holcroft would have taken more interest in the experiment than Maunsell himself and, indeed, may have had the task of assessing progress delegated to him. I think he was astute enough to realise quite early on that the benefits the equipment might have brought were outweighed by the costs of introduction and particularly of maintenance in so complicated a piece of gear.

'The class was also involved in other experiments: No 850 (NOT the LN with the same number) – by then 1850 which was fitted with Marshall valve gear in 1933 but this was a short-lived experiment as the gear failed on a trial Basingstoke–Woking working and was subsequently deemed unsuitable for use on higher-speed passenger services. Reconversion took place in April 1934. However, Maunsell did fit Marshall gear to work the inside valve on the Z class 0-8-0T.

'No 831 (renumbered 1831 by then) was on the post-war oil-burning programme, the only one of three of the class slated for conversion that actually got it, and returned to coal burning in 1948. Not experimental, of course, but the whole class was fitted with smoke deflectors from 1933. It is intriguing to know what prompted this, sixteen years after the first, No 810, had been introduced.

'One other point, this time regarding Lullingstone Airport and it never being developed as a Second World War fighter station; as the crow flies, Lullingstone is only about 6 miles from Biggin Hill, which made it ideal as a dummy. Moreover, no start had been made at all on its construction as a civilian airport before the war broke out. Heathrow, of course, had been established back in 1929. Following takeover by the RAF in 1944, the post-war Labour Government decided, very probably for financial reasons, to continue investment there for civilian purposes. This was fortunate as Lullingstone, although supposedly having the space for expansion that Croydon did not, was topographically unsuited to the sort of expansion of which Heathrow was capable, simply because much of it is on a plateau of limited size in the Darent valley. Had post-war civilian use been made at Lullingstone my house would have been right under the flightpath. I've also heard it said, by the way, that Heathrow was also favoured for development because the "nobs" lived in West London so it was quite convenient for them whereas Lullingstone was distant and awkward to get to.'

Now again some comments from Chris Sayers-Leavy on a variety of recent topics and starting with a general note about Pullman camping coaches:

'Seeing some old Pullman cars used as "camping coaches", reminded me that I went to see two of the original LB&SCR American-built Pullman coaches many years ago when I was dealing with moving rail vehicles by road at the Bluebell Railway. Having shown that we could get the cost of the road transport down by doing most of the work ourselves, we were then scouting about to see what could be recovered. The SR must have had some sort of policy about trying to sell on redundant rolling stock bodies for reuse, as grounded bodies were to be seen dotted all over the system with "virtual villages" of them at Pagham and on the Isle of White. Anyway, in a field at Partridge Green (Sussex) we found the pair of LB&SCR Pullmans, but sadly they were too far gone to be worth the cost of trying to recover them. Generally, if the bodies were structurally sound, we would jack them up and roll them on to a lorry as indeed happened with a number of four- and six-wheeled bodies that we did recovered, but the Pullmans were bogie vehicles that would originally have been "trussed" to give it the necessary longitudinal strength and the trusses had been taken off when they were "grounded", so to try to lift them would have been a bit like the *Mary Rose* recovery and well beyond our financial means.

'BR Mk1 brake picture p56, *SW33* p44, comments by Mike King. I will bow to Mike's greater knowledge on this matter. I was rather thrown by the periscope, I had not realised that so many BR Mk1s were original built with periscopes but in the light of Mike's comments I went searching through various photographs and the online archives and indeed they were there to be seen. Curiously, when I worked on SR loco-hauled rolling stock whilst at Clapham Junction shed, I don't recall ever seeing any evidence on Mk1 brake vehicles to suggest that a periscope had ever been fitted, so perhaps it was just early batches of the Mk1s that had them. The guard is certainly in a BR uniform and I saw the "livery" on the door but did not make

the connection. With regards to the guard's demeanour for an official photograph, he would not have been encouraged to look anything other than serious about his job and the picture may have been taken to demonstrate the use of the periscope to trainee staff. I'm still curious about all the "tins" stacked up on the other side of the partition?

'Straightening MN coupling rods p56, letter from Douglas Hewitt. Now I can believe almost anything said to have taken place at a running shed, especially a "remote" one, but I cannot believe that coupling rods were straightened in the manner so described. Firstly, to straighten a side rod "cold" is just inviting a further failure to occur, perhaps with even greater destruction. There would be stresses set up in the rod at the "bend" and cold straightening would only exacerbate these along with some "work hardening" of the affected area. At main Works, deformed rods would no doubt be put "under the hammer" or pressed straight and then "normalized" to remove any residual stress. I am aware that a lot of straightening used to go on, but the manner suggested also risks damaging the shed building. In most sheds the lower walls were either brickwork or concrete and those with steel uprights would have been spaced out at more than 8ft 6in centres (the length of a sleeper). These materials are very strong in compression but a lateral load even spread with a sleeper or whatever – would just cause the wall to crack. "Plate work" might have been straightened in this way, but not side rods. Even the old Longhedge works building that I used to visit regularly when we used it as a plant workshop, with its very thick brick walls, would not have taken the sort of load necessary to straighten a side rod unless it was just a "minor deflection".

'I can well imagine that hard-pressed shed staff would try most things to stop an engine going off to the Works, if they could keep it going themselves, but the risk/liability of it failing again would be very high. Better perhaps to push with a jack and timber against another loco on the adjacent line but then that could also risk damaging the other loco or even derailing it. I know that I made the previous suggestion that the quality of the steel used in the post-war era might have had something to do with these failures but I am increasingly moving away from this notion for two reasons; a) the nature of the fracture faces that I have seen where the rods actually failed as against just bending and b) the ease in which the locos could be mishandled when they "slipped". I deliberately mentioned the likely works "quality control" processes on the materials they were using, fully expecting some 'counter comments' to be raised, but neither has there been any comments as far as I am aware *(No, nothing so far – Ed.)* on the suggested ways in which the rods were manufactured or indeed why they were changed from being fluted to plain rods.

'Waterloo link line p57. My comments here may well already be known to you. But I recall reading somewhere, maybe in Dendy Marshall's volumes, that the line was only ever used for the transfer of milk traffic. Certainly the platform still exists (or at least it did as I have not been there lately). I regularly used to walk between the two stations before the high level walkway was put in and originally (1960s) you used to walk along the back of the platform, which had a wooden

The remains of No 32327 Trevithick pending a decision on its future at Eastleigh awaiting cutting up. This was the engine in charge of an evening Waterloo–Basingstoke train that collided with the rear of a Waterloo–Portsmouth electric unit just outside Woking station on 23 December 1955. Damage to No 32327 was confined to the front end and smokebox but with the few engines of this type either already, or scheduled for withdrawal, No 32327 would end its days here. Alongside are the remains of the 'odd one out', a Porter-built USA tank, WD No 1261 and never renumbered by the SR, instead being kept for spares. *John Bailey*

partition along its length to keep the public away from the open side of the platform, and the canopy was still used to keep you dry in inclement weather – the partition was really rather like a 6ft fence.

'Surviving LBSC wagons, wheel sets and their painting plus self-contained buffers, p57. Here I find Mike King's comments interesting … in my experience, the practice of painting wheel tyres white was, as much as anything in later years, just the painters "idle hands". Various handles/lettering, etc, had to be painted white (a hangover from "black out" working perhaps), whereas wheel tyres seem to have been originally painted to provide a "contrast" in "builders" black and white photographs. But given a job to paint certain items, we would often find that after this was done and perhaps rather than starting on another job, all sorts of things would be painted – usually as a matter of "looking busy" – whilst chatting. Now, I cannot for the life of me follow the logic of the different wheelbase of LBSC wagons rendering replacement wheel sets being difficult. Size for size, a replacement wheelset would fit OK, however more likely would perhaps be a larger wheel or journal diameter. Having actually rebuilt an LBSC wagon on the Bluebell (I did all the metal work on the underframe of the wagon that went to the Shildon exhibition in 1975), I cannot see the difficulty mentioned. However, there are two other factors that may have some bearing: 1. A large proportion of LBSC wagons

were on wooden underframes, which were really undesirable for general use after the Second World War with increased running speeds, heavier loading of trains and the consequent increase of power braking on goods vehicles. 2. The civil engineer would also specify a "spread" of axles (depending on their loading and wheel diameter) to maximise rail life, although I cannot see that this is particularly relevant in this case, but it just could be that the "standard" was set for the longer wheelbase size. And yes I am aware that the LBSC did have steel underframed goods stock, but a lot of these (if not all of them) were contractor-built vehicles.

'Self-contained buffers. Notwithstanding who actually originated the design of these buffers, they were also being used on the GWR, mainly on the faster running "fitted" vehicles. The earlier thin shank buffers date back to wooden underframe designs where a large horizontal leaf spring was set behind the headstock; the centre "buckle" being attached to the draw hook and the ends of the leaves providing the buffer springing. Originally the two draw hooks were not connected, other than through the wagon frame, but with heavier and heavier trains the incidence of wagons being pulled apart by rough handling and no doubt some poor maintenance, increased. Eventually the Railway Clearing House (RCH) started to produce "standard" designs of equipment, or at least the way in which the equipment functioned intended to aid necessary repairs being undertaken away from the owning companies and depots. This led to much "standardization" of many wagon "wear" parts. The large shank self-contained buffer was introduced to minimise buffer locking (the narrow shank buffers would simply bend in a collision/impact and then lock head to head against a similar failure on the adjacent vehicle) a difficult recovery to make particularly if the wagons were loaded. However, the use of continuous "draw gear" came first, with the backs of the two horizontal leaf springs mentioned above, being connected together (the wagon then effectively "floating" on the springs) and when steel underframes came to the fore, the underframes were then strong enough to take all the drawbar forces and the thin shank buffers and horizontal leaf springs could be phased out and replaced by the self-contained variety that did not buffer lock so easily. I don't doubt Mike's assertions about them being standard Maunsell/Lynes fittings but in my view as an engineer, the headstock of the van (s45682) on p46 of *SW30* was not originally "prepared" to take the larger base self-contained buffer casting. Wagon underframes tended to be assembled from "stock parts" held in store and this is the simplest explanation of the arrangement shown – if the vehicle was not refurbished or upgraded.

'Personal Bucket list – damage to 35004 p69. Firstly let me say that I have no first-hand knowledge of this failure. I am approaching the matter as an engineer and out of "curiosity", all as part of my interest in the motion failures of these engines, and as to why/how the failures occurred. As printed, the two pictures at the top of p69 are not that easy to work from, so I mainly have the article text to go on.'

Sorry, we did our best but I did say they were not of brilliant quality, however the article would not have been possible without them.

'I agree, the failure seems most likely to have arisen from a violent "slipping" incident. I also think that Eric Youldon has made the case quite well for what happened but surely it is only the leading axle to crank axle sections of the side rods that are bent and he does not explain why that might be the case. I cannot even see clearly the state of the connecting rods. Nevertheless, I agree that the damage was not caused directly by priming, but I do wonder if it might have been caused indirectly by water being "carried over". To explain, have you ever seen the regulator valve on a Bulleid Pacific? In simple terms; it is a bit like a dustbin lid, of very large proportions and quite heavy, although it is balanced by the steam pressure. I agree with Eric, a jammed regulator, and also how this is likely to have occurred. In my view, with the boiler very full of water, possibly too full (above the top nut of the gauge glass so the fireman could not determine exactly just how full the boiler was) and water was "carried over", upsetting the balance of the large regulator valve. So why did the driver not take steps to rectify the slipping as Eric outlines? I am wondering also what else might have been done that effectively caused the leading axle to stall with the other axles in "full flight", so to speak. My conclusion here has to be the use of the sanding gear. Even so, this is something of a long shot, but suppose the driver tried the

sanders (assuming that were not already being used) to get the engine to grip the rail and they didn't all work as well as the front axle set did. My only other conclusion is drawn from a note in one of your previous books *(Sorry, I am not sure which one – Ed)* about an engine being tested at Rugby; it was 35022 and the motion was reported as "whipping" at speed. Such an event suggests to me that all was not well with the design of the strength of the motion. I have long thought that at 280psi (the original boiler pressure) these engines probably developed more power than they could "put down" on the rail, certainly more than all the other SR types. Add to this their "free running" and very generously sized steam passages and balanced three-cylinder arrangement all meant that they accelerated quite rapidly, hence the propensity to slip when starting a train not handled correctly. I still don't really understand why the front set of side rods should buckle and not those at the rear end of the engine? Perhaps this has something to do with the weight transfer that takes place when hauling a train. But one way or the other the Bulleid Pacifics seem to be more prone to this type of failure than any other type of modern loco.'

I will conclude with one from Chris Duffell, which literally arrived the day I was going to send this issue off for checking:

'Another great *Southern Way* (No 36). The article on Denis Upton was interesting, especially the description of the derailment. I remember it well, as we were living in Bramley then and on the very day I was sitting with a friend in Bramley signal box chatting to Mr Hunt. It was a very very hot day! Outside Bramley signal box, in the "6ft", was a short length of rail, which had a thermometer fixed to it and it was the signalman's duty to read the temperature at regular intervals. If I recall correctly, Mr Hunt had just recorded the highest temperature reading ever taken for a length of rail. The container train concerned went through at line speed, as they normally did on that section of line. Mr Hunt watched it go out of sight around the bend, then suddenly started putting all the levers to danger. The phone rang and it was obvious something was up, as he turned to us and said, "I think you'd better get scarce, that train has come off and it's going to get rather busy around here!" Looking up the track all you could see was a cloud of dust thrown up from the ballast. We drove up the road to view the train, which looked quite normal apart from the last wagon, which was off the track, but upright. The sleepers did not look so good though as they all appeared to be cracked.

'The signal box was a standard GWR affair, which was demolished soon after, when the level crossing was converted to AHB and the ammunition depot closed (to be temporarily taken over by the Americans). Mr Hunt and the other signalmen then moved to Bramley station as ticket clerks – but they did take one memento from the box with them, the GWR signal box clock, which found further life hung in the ticket office!'

That's all for this time, but if you would like to contribute please do so either by email to editorial@thesouthernway.co.uk (preferred) or by post to the address at the start of this issue. Please note the former PO Box is no longer in use.

Fifty Years On
Counting Down to July 2017
Part Three – Spring 1967
The Photographs of Jim Seddon

Andrea Durrant

The original target day for the elimination of steam and the use of electric traction on the Bournemouth line had been 1 January 1966. Unfortunately (or fortunately dependent upon one's viewpoint) this date could not be met, one of the primary reasons being the late delivery of stock intended to replace steam. Consequently, the decision was taken to put the deadline back, first to June and then eventually to July 1967. (Even at that late stage there was an even later request to put the date back further but 'motive power' put their foot down with the statement that, having allowed steam to run down to the condition it was now in, even the limited steam diagrams would not possibly be covered. July then it had to be but which

also explains why there continued to be a hotchpotch of part-formed and culled-together sets for some months to come.

All the while though, the duties available to steam were ever being reduced but that did not stop steam seeming to be in regular use on the main line ...

Class 4 No 76066 – replete with replacement numberplate – recorded west of Wimbledon with the 11.24am Waterloo–Bournemouth holiday extra.

What may well be the Nine Elms breakdown train approaching Wimbledon from the west behind the tank equivalent of the standard 4, 2-6-4T No 80085. Nine Elms would continue to be responsible for any potential derailment requiring the use of the steam crane until 06.00 on Monday, 11 July and for which purpose a steam engine was kept at the ready in case it were needed. It was not and may well have been the last steam engine legitimately in steam on the region. After this time the crane, together with responsibility for its use, passed to the electric depot at Wimbledon.

Two morning Waterloo departures that remained steam-hauled were the 08.10 Channel Island boat train and the 08.35 Waterloo–Weymouth working. On the first of these, No 35030, formerly named Elder Dempster Line, is recorded west of Wimbledon.

Above: Jim remained in situ as on the same (unreported) day twenty-five minutes later and running exactly to time, No 35013, formerly Blue Funnel, appeared on the 08.35. The coaching stock is a mixture of loose Bulleid vehicles and BR Mk1 stock, the latter in blue/grey.

A few weeks later, Jim was at Woking to record the departure of the 08.35 west this time behind No 35007, the unnamed Aberdeen Commonwealth. The first vehicle would appear to be a catering car of BR origin in which someone else was also recording the train, this time with a reel-to-reel tape recorder.

Times were obviously bad on Thursday, February 1967 with the region being required to find engines for several boat trains, at least three special workings being scheduled to run. The third of these, featuring No 34104 Bere Alston, was seen earlier, whilst for the second train, (departing Waterloo at 10.00) all that could be mustered was Class 4 No 75074, recorded passing Vauxhall. Why the West Country should have been kept back for the third train is not known although there are several possibilities: loco availability, weight of each respective train etc, etc. At the time both Nos 34104 and 75074 were Eastleigh engines, so it is likely both had been sent ready for their respective duties.

Opposite top: The 'Kenny Belle' was the unofficial name for the steam shuttle that operated at peak times between Clapham Junction and Kensington Olympia and which remained steam-hauled until the very end. In this particular view, No 80133 is leaving Kensington Olympia for Clapham Junction with empty stock: BR 'Standard' loco; two SR Bulleid coaches (plus two BR vehicles); LNW signal cabin, and finally BR(W) lower quadrant tubular post signals. To add to the mix is a glimpse of the 1966 Motorail Terminal. Although this 'car by rail' service has been discontinued for many years, the structure still survives and is in use as one of the car parks for the adjacent Olympia exhibition hall.

Bottom: Seemingly with the same stock, this time it is an Ivatt class 2 No 41319 that is in charge as it approaches Kensington with empty stock for what will be the first of the two evening departures for Clapham Junction. This same engine had spent some time working from Eastleigh a few years before.

Here the same engine has arrived and is in the course of running round. In the background are milk tanks, another traffic regularly handled at Kensington.

Awaiting departure. Coach No S1000S is interesting, being the unique glass fibre body vehicle. Built in 1962 at Eastleigh on a second-hand underframe, this non-corridor vehicle was trialled on a number of workings including trains on the Hayling Island branch, the Lancing Belle (the workmen's train from Brighton to Lancing) and also as seen here. Following withdrawal in 1967 it was stored at Micheldever for some time before being bought for preservation on the East Somerset Railway. No S1000S (the vehicle also ran trials as DS70200 and also 1000) remains the sole railway coach built by BR and having a body of glass fibre.

A different Ivatt tank (41312) but again the same stock. This is a morning ecs departure for Clapham Junction.

An enthusiast observing trains at Kensington Olympia would be likely to witness a variety of workings. Milk, Motorail and the Clapham Junction shuttle have already been mentioned while there were regular transfer freight trips from the LMR and ER yards to the Southern freight yards south of the Thames. In addition, there were through passenger train workings. Occasionally one might also observe something even more different, London Transport steam, an example seen here with former GWR 57xx pannier tank No L90 (GWR/WR No 7760). Built in 1930 by the North British locomotive company to the standard Swindon design, No 7760 was withdrawn by BR at the end of 1961 and purchased by London Transport as one of a batch of thirteen intended to replace a number of worn-out engines. Renumbered as L90 and now sporting red LT livery, several continued in use until steam was finally retired from the London Transport lines in the early 1970s. No L90 has a train of rails proceeding in the direction of Willesden.

A foretaste of things to come in the final instalment of Jim Seddon's images to appear in the July issue. A brace of Standard Class 4 tanks, Nos 80143 and 80140 have come off the turntable at Nine Elms and are being shunted into their required position. It would appear as if the lead engine is not in steam. In the background No 34108, formerly carrying the name Wincanton awaits its place on the turntable.

Main Line Fireman
Former Nine Elms Fireman Bill Berry
Interviewed by David Vaughan in 2016

H15 No 30489 at Nine Elms. *Roger Thornton*

Bill Berry was born in 1931 and lived in Lavender Hill, where his father had a fish shop. On the outbreak of war he was evacuated to Northampton where, having completed schooling under what were difficult wartime conditions, he left and went to work in a shoe factory.

When peace was restored, he returned to the family home to work in the family shop. Initially this went well but in late 1945 he was visited by a school board inspector who enquired who he was. On discovering that Bill was just 14 years old and had no formal school leaving certificate, he enquired about his future prospects. Asking, 'What are you going to do my lad?' With a laugh Bill replied, 'I want to be an engine driver.' 'Well,' said a well-informed inspector, 'it's no laughing matter, but if you want to be an engine driver you have to sign on as a cleaner first and work your way up. If you're serious, come and see me tomorrow and I will give you a letter of introduction to the shed superintendent at Nine Elms.'

DV: This visit marked the beginning of what was destined to be a relatively short but eventful career on the Southern Railway but also coinciding with a period of great change on the railways. I went to interview Bill at his home in Bexhill-on-Sea and initially asked him how he had got on during that first visit to Nine Elms.

BB: On the following Monday morning I went and reported to the shed superintendent Mr Maitland* and, along with about eight other lads, was started as a cleaner. After about four weeks, a chap with a bowler hat and a briefcase came along and asked us a few questions about how to go about preparing an engine and what equipment to use, which by then I was able to answer. Evidently my answer had been satisfactory because about three months later he came back again and asked a lot more questions, this time covering things such as signalling and the technique for firing a locomotive. Again I was able to answer all the questions so he said I was now a passed cleaner, meaning I was able to go on locomotive firing duties.**

I reported to Nine Elms goods yard and spent some time there learning the art of firing on various Drummond locomotives, ironically the driver I was with was also named Berry, although no relation. Again after a while the same bowler-hatted inspector returned and after a further question and answer session, I was passed out as a fireman. I went to the stores at London Bridge to collect my uniform and at Nine Elms was put straight into number 48 link classified as a spare link intended to cover crews on everything from light shunting to the prestige Atlantic Coast Express ('ACE') and the Southampton boat trains.

DV: As a passed fireman I don't suppose you saw much of those trains at first?

BB: Certainly not, those duties would have been allocated to the senior spare men. My duties were still mainly on shunting and goods trains but if you were the only one available it could be anything, even a junior man on a mainline passenger turn. I remember going to Waterloo for the first time and seeing the boat trains waiting in the centre road with about twelve Pullman cars all with headboards carrying the name of the boat they were destined for – *Queen Mary* and such like. I would watch the passengers and the porters loaded with suitcases and trunks at the same time wondering if I would ever get to go on the footplate of one of these top link trains.

DV: So, as a cleaner, did you have any connection with the locomotives you were allocated to on these prestigious trains?

BB: When the Bournemouth Belle started running again and with a new Merchant Navy class in charge, the shed foreman came up to us cleaners and said, 'Right I want you to go into that coal truck and break up all the big lumps with a pick ready to go in the tender of the engine on the Belle.' Our instructions were that no piece of coal was to be larger than a man's fist otherwise they might block the tender doors and cause difficulties in maintaining the schedule – on the Belle this was tight. Eventually this amount of preparation was stopped.

As cleaners we cleaned engines, of course, whilst if times were slack or if it was a very important job then, even as a passed fireman, we might be tasked with assisting. One such example was when an engine was being prepared for a Royal duty and I remember having to do not one but two Lord Nelson-class engines at one time. They had to be in tip-top condition, of course, with the buffers all quartered up and all the motion looking like new: two engines as one was kept as the reserve.

There was a charge hand called Harry Harris who had been a fire lighter. In his day he used to go to the sand drier, which had a fire under it all the time, get a shovel full of burning coals, put it over his shoulder and then climb on to the footplate of the engine, where he had already placed some kindling wood in the firebox. The contents of the shovel was then tipped into the firebox to be followed by small pieces of coal. He would continue this way, gradually adding more and more coal until it was almost up to the firehole door.

In the cleaner grade, if we were tasked to help, we had a chore even before the kindling had been added to the firebox. This was to go to a large bin coincidentally located next to the sand drier that contained beach pebbles. We collected a shovelful of pebbles and scattered them over the empty fire bars. When the engine was under way from Waterloo the driver opened the regulator and the fire that had been built up at the back would lift with the force of the blast shooting over the bars and remaining pebbles. The fireman would get

Above: **Bill and his driver on No 34061 73 Squadron. A poor quality image but historically important.**

Bill's [? I assume this is not Bill] driver at Nine Elms. (We regret efforts to provide a name have proven unsuccessful.)

the pricker out and help to spread the coal so that by the time you got to say, Clapham Junction, there was a nice even fire ready for the faster sections ahead. The idea was that the pebbles would let air through to give draught to the new fire and would also stop clinker clogging up the firebars.

As a junior I always seemed to get the job of filling the sandboxes on the engine. We also had to fill two oil cans one with thick and the other thin oil, both drawn from the stores, and top up the wicks on any engine with inside motion. Officially this was the job of the driver but we were expected to do as we were tasked. That job meant getting underneath the engine to sit on the inside motion, which was a bit cramped to say the least. Also, by this time the fire was burning through so certain parts were hot. The tops of the oil pots had corks in them and also a cane through them to let the air in and prevent an air lock.

DV: What are your memories of your early days on the footplate?

BB: I remember that my dad was so proud of the fact that I had passed out as a fireman that he used to come with my little brother to the railings at Spencer Park when he knew I was on the footplate and wave to me as we passed.

To start with though I worked mainly on the Drummond tanks. These were mainly the M7s, used for pulling empty carriage stock mainly between the sidings at Clapham Junction and Waterloo. We pulled the coaches for the Bournemouth Belle, the Devon Belle plus the boat trains, the various Pullman cars having come up from Stewarts Lane.

On spare duties we had to go and 'square up' the engines booked for the express trains, which meant that we would walk from Nine Elms to Vauxhall and then take a train to Waterloo. When a train, say from Bournemouth came in, the main line crew would go off duty to the mess room and we would take the engine back to Nine Elms ready to turn, replenish the coal and water and then take it back to Waterloo tender first ready for its next duty, sometimes with the same men who had brought it in. We did this up to three times per shift. This was the way I got to know about all the different types of engines.

I quickly found the firebox doors on the Merchant Navy and West Country/Battle of Britain types were nice and big and operated by a foot treadle. You would open the door, put a shovel full of coal down the middle, the door would close, then repeat the process one on the left and one on the right, and finally close the door again. We would also turn the empty shovel over to deflect the glare and this enabled you to see where any holes in the fire might be that could otherwise affect steaming. The King Arthur and Lord Nelson classes had smaller fireholes and when I started firing to these I often hit the backhead instead with the shovel, especially if the engine was rolling about a bit. Then, of course, there was coal all over the floor, which did not please the driver at all.

I remember one driver, his name was Joe Wolf, who always wore a spotlessly clean pair of blue overalls. When I was coupling up at Waterloo he would go through the carriages and collect the old newspapers to sit on in the cab and I had

to use the pep pipe to hose down the footplate on his side do he didn't get any coal dust on him. I remember that, as we were going up from Clapham on the way to Vauxhall, he used to recite this poem;

The headlight shone out through the darkness, the train thundered along on the rails.

Rapidly sped the huge engine pulling the limited mails.

The fireman looked up from his furnace, his face was cheerful and bright,

he looked at his mate on the throttle and said, 'I'm meeting her, Jim, tonight.'

I don't know where he got that from but he often used to sing it out loud as we were going along. I used to wonder what he was about but I think he must have been remembering his days on the top-link expresses as he had served his time and was now back on the tank engines.

Other drivers I remember were Percy Cox, on the 6pm Salisbury run, Ernie Harvey, on the Atlantic Coast Express and 'boiler buster' Hopkins, who never pulled the throttle lever back unless he had to. Locally we used to do a run to Chertsey with a fish train and I recall we sometimes had a lovely engine on that turn. This was No 119, a T9 and the old Royal engine. It was kept in beautifully lined passenger green livery but was used on the fish train to keep it in running order in case it was needed on a special.

During my time on the spare I eventually did get to fire on the 'ACE' and the down 6pm Waterloo to Salisbury train. If we were on the latter we would arrive at Salisbury, uncouple and go on shed to have our break. The Salisbury shed gang would then prepare our engine for the return trip, which was the 10.15pm milk train up from Devon with a load of about fifteen milk tankers. We hauled these as far as Clapham Junction from where a Drummond tank engine would take the tanks to the Express Dairy depot at Vauxhall Bridge, hauling about five or six at a time, and then bring empties back.

DV: Of course, if you started work on the railways in 1945 you witnessed the changeover when the railways were nationalised in 1948. How did that seem to you?

BB: One thing I do remember was when they had the locomotive exchanges and we had *Mallard* on shed at Nine Elms [see Image 5]. My driver, who was also a deputy shed foreman at the time, and myself were allocated to go with the LNER crew to Waterloo where a pilot driver would be waiting for the engine to take it on a train to Salisbury with the LNER crew. I remember on the short journey the 'foreigners' showed me through the corridor tender and although we were only acting as pilots ourselves I got the opportunity to put some coal in the firebox, hence I can genuinely lay claim to having fired *Mallard*!

At the time the tenders on the West Country and Merchant Navy were still all green and smartly lined out, but those of our engines intended for the trials and so likely to be sent 'off region' were given plain black tenders from the Midland but which had water scoops fitted, Most of these were simply labelled 'British Railways' on the sides. At Nine Elms, the Bulleid engines could, when clean, look very smart. We were given platforms to stand on to clean these engines and took a pride in turning them out looking their best. It took some time after nationalisation to change the livery and numbers from SR to BR lined passenger green. They used to go down to Eastleigh two or three at a time and come back later with the new livery applied.

One year (1947) there was a big exhibition at Waterloo and I fired one of the engines going to it, which was *Boxhill*. It was in what they called Stroudley improved engine green livery but it looked more like yellow or orange to me!

DV: Do you remember any particular incidents during your time on the footplate?

BB: One incident I do remember was with a West Country class engine on a passenger train. We had gone through Clapham Junction and were coming up to Earlsfield. Now we were told never to fire going through a station to avoid smoke, so when I did open the firehole door shortly afterwards I could not believe my eyes, the fire had literally disappeared. I frantically gestured to the driver to come and look and what we saw was that most of the fire bars had dropped through and I was in effect firing into the ashpan. The driver sounded the emergency signal on the whistle 'Cock-a-doodle-do' and he wrote a note on a scrap of paper and tied it to a lump of coal with a piece of oil wick and threw it out at the next signal box, alerting the signalman that we had a problem. There were still some firebars remaining at the sides of the firebox so I fired as best I could and we got through to Basingstoke, where we were stopped. We were expecting a relief loco and to go on shed to drop the fire but there was evidently nothing available and instead we were told to continue but not as per the schedule to stop at Andover, and instead come off at Salisbury, which we did. They were all waiting for us and, as soon as we uncoupled and got over the pit at the loco shed, I had to go underneath with a pick and knock the ashpan off and drop the fire, which was, of course, full of a lot of very hot fire. I got out of there a bit sharpish and we quickly backed the engine off the pit. How we had got that far in that state I do not know but the driver later told me he could hear the oil in the oil bath for the chain drive bubbling.

The tender on an engine is, of course, connected by the drawbar, which is sprung and I remember that, on the King Arthur type in particular, there was a tendency for this fall plate to jump about a bit; in fact one man on the Salisbury run had a nasty accident on the move when he was shovelling coal forward and the fall plate jumped up and somehow he caught his foot under it. It came down on him and his foot was badly injured.

One of the first main line runs I did was on the 5.45 all stops to Salisbury. This was on a King Arthur and I started the trip by pulling some coal forward but the driver stopped me and said, 'Don't do that – there is no need.' He went on to instruct me sternly, 'Just keep an even fire and nurse it along gently.' Well, we hadn't got as far as Woking when there was coal all over the footplate. Such was the movement of the tender with all

the stopping and starting that the coal I had pulled down had already come forward too far. I had to clear it away and hose the footplate down.

I had another rather nasty experience on the same type of engine as we were going over the junction at Woking where the electrified lines to Portsmouth went off. As we went bouncing over the junction points the pricker bar on the tender jumped up out of its holder. I thought it was going over the side and might land on the live rail so I instinctively reached up to grab it but the spike on the end went right into my hand. It was, if I remember rightly, driver Hopkins and having seen what had happened, he stopped the train. After conferring with the guard and signalman we propelled back into Woking station, a highly unorthodox move, but the driver had seen how bad my injury was. Anyway at Woking they said, 'We can't get a relief fireman here, you will have to go on to Basingstoke,' so they bandaged my hand as best they could and tied my arm across my chest. Of course, I could not fire the engine in that state so the driver fired all the way to Basingstoke whilst I watched out for the signals. By the time we got to Basingstoke the blood had soaked through the bandage so they got me off and were going to send me straight to hospital but just then the Royal Mail train came in going to Waterloo and I was put on that and entrusted to the care of the guard. I will always remember him, he was a lovely old boy, took care of me and retied my bandage. When we got to Waterloo I went straight to St Thomas's Hospital and was subsequently off work for three weeks. I went back on light duties for a couple of weeks after that until my hand healed up.

On occasions a film crew would take over the railway. I remember, although I wasn't involved, when they filmed *Passport to Pimlico* that they had an electric train made ready in Platform 1 at Vauxhall and a load of film extras on the platform. They were all given parcels and when they got to the certain bridge they had to throw them over to the people below, who in the film had declared Pimlico an independent state, in order to break the blockade imposed by the authorities.

Another time I had to get an engine ready that they were going to use in a film. We put it over in one corner of the yard at Nine Elms and the director had the people running about all over the tracks in some sort of chase scene, which they later speeded up and put in the film. They certainly could not do that sort of thing on the main line, hence the use of the yard. I don't know what film it was though. *(Can any reader help here – Ed?)*

The Bulleid Pacifics were, as you may know, prone to slipping and when you were under the gantry at Waterloo with the through signal off and twelve or thirteen bogies tied on to the tender, you would be hard-pressed to get out of the station unless you had the assistance of the tank engine on the back that had brought the empty stock in. The Pullman trains were the heaviest.

When you got past Earlsfield you had a nice run down to Woking and then there was a short covered way. The driver would put his hand out across the footplate to let you know what was coming up; this gave time to close the firehole door or else there was the danger of getting a blowback.

Bulleid Merchant Navy No 35021 New Zealand Line in original form – save for the cut-down tender – and Standard 5 No 73089 later named Maid of Astolat. A number of Class 5s were transferred to the Southern Region in the 1950s to take over the roles previously undertaken by members of the Urie King Arthur class, some names from the latter also being transferred to the former. Also note the tender of 73089 where the coal space has been partitioned. This was a feature of several standard locomotives working on the Southern Region and was to ensure route axle weights were not exceeded when carrying a full tank of water. The location is Nine Elms.

Now I should explain that when you went to sign on and collect your gear they always gave you what they called a green liner. It was a cleaning rag with a green line through to show it was SR property and that was what you used to wipe the sweat and oil off your face. When you took it back at the end of a shift it was put in the wash, so we always got a clean one. We also got two other rags for general cleaning. Anyway, I never did like tunnels so I was always looking out for the light at the other end. This particular time I was on a boat train, with, I think, a Lord Nelson. As we came out of the tunnel, I said to the driver, with some alarm in my voice, 'Something's burning!' I looked round to see what it was only to discover that the green liner in my own pocket had caught a spark off the fire whilst in the tunnel and I was well alight!

DV: I understand that you had a break in service with the railways in the late 1940s. Is that right?

BB: In 1949, having worked at Nine Elms for only three years, I was called up for National Service. After initial training and a period as a regimental cook I was sent to the Longmoor Military Railway. When I proudly announced on arrival that I was by now a passed fireman the officer in charge said, 'Oh no not another ruddy fireman, I wanted a driver!' Unfortunately it was not an engine driver he wanted but a lorry driver. I told him I had driving experience with my father's van so I found myself on an Austin 3-ton truck delivering spare track parts, parts for turnouts, rail chairs, etc. to all the many Army bases that had railway sidings. After I had finished my National Service I returned to work at Nine Elms but, in the meantime my parents had moved to Banstead and the travelling to and from the depot by train took up so much time that it was almost the situation that when I arrived home it was time for bed ready for an early start the next day. So it was that I only did another year on the railway and reluctantly gave in my notice to start another career with the London ambulance service. I recall my last day on the railway working with Driver Ernie Harvey. We had gone down to Salisbury on the 'ACE' with a West Country class and come back to Clapham Junction as passengers. Ernie complimented me on my firing and gave me a packet of twenty cigarettes as a parting gift.

*This was John Pelham Maitland, who was born in Croydon on 31 March 1890 and died in Haywards Heath in July 1964. J. P. Maitland had started as a premium apprenticeship under Douglas Earle Marsh on 4 January 1907. He was in charge of the sheds at Newhaven (from 1924), at Littlehampton and Bognor (from 1929), at the new mpd at Norwood Junction from 1935, and was Running Shed Superintendent at Nine Elms from 1939 until his retirement. He was one of the founders of the Institution of Locomotive Engineers and presented four early papers. He was awarded the MBE for his work in assisting the dispersal of the troops from Dunkirk. According to Fred Rich, author of *Yesterday Once More: a Story of Brighton Steam* (Bromley: P. E. Waters & Associates, 1996), Maitland was an excellent linguist and highly competent archaeologist. Maitland was also a founder Member of the Institution of Locomotive Engineers and presented its first (in 1912) and thirteenth (in 1913) papers. (Biographical details from *Steam Index*.)

** By implication this was a very short time from starting as a cleaner to being allowed out as a 'passed cleaner' and then indeed later to the full 'fireman' grade. We may take it there was a hangover of shortages of footplate crews at this time.

Last Train to Blandford Forum

Following withdrawal of regular S&D line passenger services in March 1966, Blandford Forum continued to see freight traffic until January 1969, when final closure came. *Jeffery Grayer* recalls the handful of passenger specials that traversed the route from Broadstone Junction to the Dorset market town during this period

As darkness fell on the evening of Saturday, 5 March 1966 the final scheduled passenger services left Blandford Forum station on the Somerset & Dorset line. By this time the infamous Interim Emergency Service was in operation, consisting of just a handful of trains in each direction. The last northward service was the 19.34 to Bath Green Park, which was so delayed by 'last rites' and the number of passengers wishing to travel that it reached Bath some fifty minutes late. The final southbound departure was the 21.39 to Bournemouth Central, the traditional S&D terminus of Bournemouth West having been closed six months previously. Additionally, there had been two enthusiast specials operated by the LCGB and the GWS, the former passing

The last passenger service to arrive at Blandford was headed by electro-diesel E6108 top and tailed with Class 47 D1986 at the rear of the train for the return journey. The train was the LCGB Hampshireman special of 3 November 1968, scheduled to depart Blandford at 16.15 following a twenty-minute stop. The Class 74 had headed the train on the outgoing run, which had started from Waterloo that morning and proceeded via Guildford and Cosham to Fareham. There D6506 took over for a trip on the Gosport branch followed by a visit to the Fawley branch. On arrival back at Totton, E6108 took over for the run to Poole, where it was joined on the rear by D1986. Following a foray up the Blandford stub, D1986 assumed sole charge for the return to Waterloo via Alresford and Ascot. This had not been the first appearance of a Class 74 on the line, for in April/May 1968 they had been noted on the freight service to Bailey Gate on at least two occasions. However, this was probably the first time that they had penetrated as far as Blandford. *Author*

through Blandford just before 18.00 unforgettably hauled by two unrebuilt Bulleid Pacifics. The following day there were a couple of specials, there being no Sunday service on the S&D, the first heading northwards, making a five-minute stop at Blandford about 13.30 crossing with the southbound special, with the final northbound return leg reaching the Georgian market town just before 17.00. That should have been it as far as passengers were concerned as there now remained merely a freight service southwards to Broadstone Junction.

Although not known at the time, the LCGB tour illustrated above was to be the final passenger train to operate from Blandford a couple of months before complete closure of the remaining freight-only stub of the former S&D mainline. Following closure to regular passenger trains on 6 March 1966, Blandford was to see a handful of passenger specials over the next 2¾ years. The first reappearance of coaching stock was on 21 May 1966, barely two months after formal closure, when the Southern region's unique Standard Class 3 No 77014 was seen with the British Young Traveller Society special of 21 May

1966, arriving at Blandford's up platform, rather than the down that was officially the only one in use at this time, No 77014 had to run round its four-coach train to work tender first back to Broadstone.

The following month, on 6 July 1966, 34012 *Launceston* had charge of a nine- coach special for workers at the local brewery Hall & Woodhouse. The destination was Brighton. Brewing of beer had been a local industry since 1777, when an enterprising Charles Hall started brewing for the troops stationed in Weymouth to counter the growing French threat across the Channel. The brewery is currently owned by the seventh generation of the Woodhouse family and it had a long tradition of organising an outing by rail for the workforce. In 1968, on 15 June, a final rail outing was scheduled but this time, following the end of steam on the SR on 9 July 1967, the train was diesel-hauled by Crompton D6540. The destination on this occasion was Kew but as arrival back in Poole was at night the special was barred from returning to Blandford so passengers had to board road coaches to finish their trip.

Ivatt tank No 41320 has just arrived at Blandford with the Manchester Rail Travel Society special of 25 March 1967. *Derek Fear*

Storming down the perceptible grade through the former Charlton Marshall halt, closed in 1956, No 77014 is at the head of the returning special of 16 October 1966. *Derek Fear*

Between these brewery excursions another couple of enthusiast specials operated, the first on 16 October 1966. This was topped and tailed by Standards Nos 77014 with 76026 hauling the LCGB special The Dorset & Hants railtour. I vividly recall watching this pass at Bailey Gate crossing on the A31, where a long tailback of cars was hampered by numerous parked vehicles, their occupants eager to see the passing spectacle of five coaches and two locomotives. 76026 was at the front for the journey to Blandford while 77014 led on the return journey as far as Poole, where the train reversed for a trip down the Hamworthy Goods line. The tour had previously visited the Ringwood line with the two Standards.

The second railtour involved Ivatt tank No 41320 which worked the Hants & Dorset Branch Flyer. This was billed as the last steam hauled tour over the Blandford line, which with the end of SR steam fast approaching, did indeed prove to be the case. Originating at Southampton, the tour began with USA haulage in the shape of No 30064 to Fawley, being

relieved at Totton on the return by No 80151, which took a trip down the Lymington branch. On return to Brockenhurst, the tour recommenced with the Ivatt in charge for a trip up to Blandford and return, followed by an outing on the Swanage branch.

BR announced the withdrawal of the remaining freight service to Bailey Gate, where milk traffic had been handled, and to Blandford with effect from 6 January 1969. The final scheduled freight ran on 2 January with Crompton No 6513 in charge, leaving just a few remaining wagons awaiting collection at Blandford some days later. Track was left in situ for almost a year before lifting began at the end of December 1969, a process that continued until September 1970 when Broadstone Junction was reached by the demolition crews. In the words of the famous Flanders & Swann comic song *The Slow Train*, 'No more will I go to Blandford Forum and Mortehoe … '

Displaying headcode 1Z13 green-liveried Brush Type 4 No D1986 prepares to leave Blandford with the last ever passenger service, the LCGB special of 3 November 1968. A few weeks later Blandford lost its surviving freight service and so 105 years after the opening of the station in September 1863 it ceased to be a railway-served town. D1986, introduced to traffic in January 1966, was scrapped in November 1999. *Author*

No 76026 heads the LCGB special of 16 October with No 77014 bringing up the rear approaching Corfe Mullen gates with the former Wimborne line seen on the left. *Derek Fear*

A view from the bridge overlooking the station showed some evidence, in the goods yard behind the signal box, of goods traffic being carried in 1967. However, the only regular items by this time comprised coal and fertiliser with some hops for the local brewery and occasional specials for the Army at nearby Blandford Camp. Parcels traffic, which had continued to be handled after March 1966, was finally dispensed with in January 1967. The remaining goods could be carried comfortably by a couple of trains per week. As this shot was taken on 9 July 1967, the last day of SR steam, the surviving platform end water crane complete with bag would no longer be required. *Author*

Memories of happier times at Blandford are recalled with No 92209 with the Southern Counties Touring Society special The South Western Rambler of 8 March 1964. The tour had started at Waterloo with Britannia Pacific No 70020 Mercury in charge as far as Salisbury, where the 2-10-0 took over for the run from [to?] Bournemouth via Templecombe. Notwithstanding an itinerary that included a trip up the remains of the former MSWJ from Andover as far as Ludgershall, together with the inherent shunting at Andover and Templecombe, the train was ten minutes early arriving at Blandford. There advantage was taken with an extended photo stop. The service remained slightly early until time was lost in the vicinity of Redbridge on the return and Waterloo was reached ten minutes behind time.

What's in a Picture?

Chris Sayers-Leavy

Thumbing through the most recent copy of *SW36*, my eye was drawn to the pictures on p73 and in particular the middle view showing the back of an L1 tender and the broken axle that has caused the derailment. My initial reaction was that the picture had been printed in reverse but on closer examination I could see that that the engine number was printed the correct way round and this then got me wondering.

Well, there is nothing particularly unusual about the failure/derailment but look again and you will notice that the steam heat pipe is in the wrong position, or at least I should

say perhaps that it is not in the conventional position, being as it is to the left-hand side of the draw hook. Now most people around today, who have done any coupling up of

This is the only image I have been able to find that does indeed show that in SECR ownership the steam heating connection – just the pipe end and cock are visible in the view (the hose has been taken off) was located on the left-hand side of the coupling hook. The incident was a collision at St Johns in 1898 and displays to devastating effect the risk from 'telescoping' of wooden-bodied vehicles. The brake van body, despite becoming completely detached from its underframe, remains virtually intact. (See Southern Way Special No 8 for more information on this accident)

The image referred to from p73 of SW36. As viewed, the vacuum brake pipe is on the right and the non-standard heating hose connection on the left side of the drawhook. (Full captions details relevant to the broken axle are in the issue to which Chris refers.) *S. C. Townroe*

coaching stock, will know that the steam heat pipe is located on the right-hand side of a loco's buffer beam between the draw hook and the buffer. Not only that but it can be an absolute pig to couple up as of necessity to withstand the pressure and temperature they work at, these items are very stiff and unyielding to any human effort being applied to try to connect two of them together! By the modern convention of being on the right-hand side of the draw hook – the one on the vehicle being coupled up also being in that position – the two pipe ends come together under the coupling. They then interlock on one side and by applying some downward pressure the joint closes, the two hinged hooks are then closed (sometimes with the aid of the coal hammer) to make good the 'joint'. Now trying to connect up these steam heating pipes when they are both on the same side of the coupling must have been a real struggle, if indeed it could be done at all. By comparison, the vacuum brake pipes are different, more flexible and, being originally located, at the end of a 'swan neck' stand pipe, they naturally hang down or 'fall' roughly in alignment. These are then joined above the coupling, with an

interlocking 'tail' that forms part of their connection. The pipes are again closed by pulling down on the joint to bring them together and then inserting a spring clip into one of the interleaving 'tongues' to keep the joint closed. So I naturally wondered why was the pipe on the L1 tender, in the position that it was ...? As I have just compiled another explanatory piece for Kevin Robertson, an idea came into my mind and this then sent me scurrying off to trawl through other back issues of *SW* to look for more clues to this mystery.

Now I have often wondered why, after the amalgamation of the three main constituent companies that made up the Southern in 1923, there was not a greater mixing of the various locos and rolling stock that the Southern inherited than occurred. The LBSCR, having settled on Westinghouse air brakes for its stock, was an obvious oddity, compared to the other two companies that had both opted for vacuum brakes (the LCDR had been air-braked prior to its amalgamation with the SER, which resulted in the SECR) unless dual fitted, whilst it follows LBSCR locomotives and rolling stock could not be used with the alternative vacuum braking system. But steam heating, surely

Steam heating pipe   Vacuum brake pipe

Here we see the normal arrangement of hose connections used before the introduction of coaches having corridor connections and which in many cases lasted right up to the end of steam. The pipes are mounted in the same position on each vehicle and thus when brought together they take up a position approx 45° to the ends and are kept clear of the haulage coupling. Early variations of this layout sometimes 'angled' the swan neck vacuum pipe towards the centre line of the vehicles – this being a 'neutral axis' that incurred the minimum movement of the pipe as the train progressed along the track.

they all used steam heating? As it turns out, I did not have to look too far as all the images that I viewed of ex-SECR locos on passenger trains taken in the early years of the Southern had the steam heating pipes in the same location. So by deduction alone it would appear that the SECR must have had a different company standard to the LBSCR and the LSWR. This is a difference I was unaware of up until now. The 'proof' of this for me would be to find some pictures of the ends of SE&CR coaching stock with an arrangement that matches their locos, but such a clear illustration has been very hard to find … Incidentally, the picture of a SECR 4-4-0 at the top of p61 in *SW36* illustrates the same arrangement as that described above for SECR locos but the steam heating pipe has been removed from the shut off cock, I wonder why? As this is a quite a late (BR) picture, the days of the engine being required to steam heat a train whilst running backwards were no doubt well behind it and by some considerable number of years.

With the introduction of corridor connections on coaching stock, the tall swan neck vacuum brake pipes on locomotives could no longer be used as they had to be connected under the haulage coupling rather than above it and a variety of different pipe mountings were used, some just appearing under the buffer beams and others using a shorter swan neck pipe, although the standard that emerged was for the brake hose to be on the left-hand side of the draw hook, with the steam heating pipe being located in a similar position on the right-hand side. Thus when coupled, the connections 'lay' at 90° to one another under the coupling. So it would appear that the SECR standard was then the opposite of what was required. It would, of course, still be possible and easy to couple up a SECR loco to SE&CR coaches but it must have been quite difficult, if even possible to couple to vehicles having the steam heating pipe on the same side.

Interestingly it seems that a greater priority was given to modifying the tenders/rear of tank engines as there are plenty of example of ex SECR locos retaining the old arrangement at the front of the engine, right up to the end of steam. A point of interest is that the early LMS prototype diesels also had the 'reversed' pipe arrangement which must have made the fireman struggle to couple up.

Note – Two points from the editorial desk to perhaps add slightly to the above. Firstly, loco crews no doubt quickly became adept at coupling an engine and coach as a point of necessity, although it was a skill that had to be mastered. Harold Gasson in his book *Firing Days* (OPC-1973) speaks of his own first firing turn on a passenger train that was booked for the following day but preceded the afternoon before with two hours private instruction from the shunter in 'the art of tying an engine to a coach'. Harold adds this cost him the price of a couple of pints later that evening. More serious is why the Railway Clearing House and/or the Association of Locomotive Engineers did not attempt to unify the coupling hose arrangements? Perhaps even such differences occurred on other companies' lines and with their own respective absorbed stock as well?

Guildford to Winchester
The Facts and the Forgotten

The name Denis Cullum should be familiar to many readers. Sadly no longer with us, Denis was a career railwayman not on the operational side but instead a collector (perhaps the term 'hoarder' would be more appropriate – although intended in the nicest possible way) who used his position within the Rules office at Waterloo to amass a vast repository of historical documentation on lines throughout the Southern. In the same manner as such gentlemen as Reg Randall and Derek Clayton in the Waterloo Plan Arch (ably encouraged by Doug Stephenson, their supervisor at Croydon), he assisted many a researcher during his working life, and indeed continues to do so.

Another name that must be mentioned, so far as the Denis Cullum archive is concerned, is that of Neville Bridger. Neville was not a railwayman, his own career involving science, but be will be better known to many as having operated the Marlborough Railway bookshop for many years. This is sadly no more but not, I hasten to add, through the choice of Neville

himself. I had known Denis for many years, visiting him several times at his home in Alton. He had a room dedicated to his archive, which, although I did not know it at the time, included a specific file on many actual routes. Whilst the hundreds (thousands) of photographs taken by Denis are fortunately available once more through the Lens of Sutton Association, I was unaware his 'line archives' (or at least some) ended up with Neville, and it was through a chance conversation that this became apparent accompanied by the words, 'Would you like them on loan?' Now who was I to refuse and so as a start let us begin with 'Guildford to Winchester Junction'. I should add that we do not have a file on every route, whilst some consist literally of a single sheet with the name of the railway and nothing else. This then is the first we shall feature, others will follow in due course.

Thirty to forty years later and Ropley is now unstaffed, the siding has been removed and trains pause briefly to and from Alton. But the topiary is still present … *Rod Hoyle*

Gas lighting at Alresford survived (we think) right up to closure in February 1973. A evening view in what was indeed the evening of services on the railway under public ownership. *Edward Griffiths*

Denis's notes and papers are very much laid out in factual form more as a series of notes or aide-memoire, the same format being used here. Unless otherwise stated, the images used are from various other sources, the files bereft of actual photographs.

Ash Vale – Farnham Junction. Formed part of the Guildford to Winchester Junction branch of LSWR.

Opened: Guildford to Ash Junction on 20th August 1849, Ash Junction to Farnham on 8th October 1849. Subsequently Farnham to Alton on 28th July 1852, and Alton to Winchester Junction on 8th October 1865. Ash Junction to Farnham via Tongham closed to passenger traffic on 4th July 1937.

Ash Green: originally opened as Ash, but renamed in December 1876, reverted to Ash in September 1891. Reverted again to Ash Green on 1st October 1895. Unstaffed and renamed Ash Green Halt 1st December 1926, closed to goods on same date.

Tongham: opened October 1956. Closed to passengers 4th July 1937. Closed to goods 2nd January 1961. (Suggestion part may have been retained for a short time afterwards to serve the Aldershot Gas Co. sidings.)

Signalling, Ash Junction. Layout altered 13th September 1936. Signal alterations in connection with key-token working between Ash Junction and Farnham Junction, 9th February 1930. At Tongham the signal box was abolished, up platform (to Guildford) taken out of use and all down and up trains to use down (to Winchester) platform with intermediate key token instrument for the sidings (with shut-away facilities). Conversion of double line into single line between Ash Junction and Farnham Junction. Up line at Tongham converted into a siding with buffer stops 327 yards Farnham side and 537 yards Ash side of station respectively.

The file then gives details of various alterations/changes/installations/operational workings etc referring to specific locations. Clearly over a time span of 100+ years a collection of some sixteen papers (plus some drawings and operational notes) cannot hope to cover the full history of this railway but even so, what Denis has managed to collate is material that might otherwise have been lost or remained moribund.

Starting then with the installation of a telephone at Deer Barn Bridge (between Guildford and Wanborough), and a memorandum from the E. J. Sharpe, Traffic Manager, in the London West Divisional Superintendents office, dated 26 September 1934. 'Emergency Telephone. A cupboard, painted with black and white diagonal stripes is fixed on the Up side of the line on a telegraph post on the Guildford side of Deer Barn Bridge, which is situated between Guildford and Wanborough stations. This contains a telephone connected with the Shalford signal box–North Camp signal box circuit. This telephone is provided to enable trainmen to communicate with the Signalman in case of emergency.'

Pinks Hill – From Henry Holmes, District Superintendent's Office, Waterloo, 7th December 1904. 'Proposal to remove the Signal Box to the Level Crossing so that the signalman could control the gates – similar to the arrangement we are making at Arnolds' Crossing at Eastleigh. Pringle inspected 20th

Exterior of Ash Green, 16 March 1957. *S. W. C. Eyers collection*

January 1910. Gates opened by hand and do not close across the railway. Signal Box contains six levers, all in use.

'Auto half-barriers provided Mar/Apr 1967. Originally proposed for "on-call" barriers but these refused by only regular user who lived in nearby house.' Denis adds without elaboration, 'A great shindig.' 'On the up line was an automatic colour light signal and this necessitated special instruction under failure conditions (of the barriers). SB reduced to Gate Box 13/2/1966. Auto half-barriers abolished 28/6/71 alternative roadway constructed, cost £12,000 estimated. Bridle crossing with one bridle gate each side, one whistle board in each direction. (Resulted from Hixon modifications of AHB's – cost of alterations, £12,600.'

Ministry of Transport, 19 February 1932. Col A. C. Trench. 'I have the honour to report for the information of the Minister of Transport that, in accordance with the appointment of the 22th December 1930, I made an inspection of 18th February 1932, of the new works in connection with the singling of the line between Ash Junction and Farnham Junction on the Southern Railway.

'This line, formerly double, has been reduced to single line by the removal of the majority of the old up track and the provision of new junctions immediately inside the double line junctions at either end. At these points also various alterations have been made to the signalling and to the normal lie of the main junction points, as indicated on the drawings.' (*The drawings referred to do not accompany the file – Ed.*)

'The line is now worked on the key-token system with one token section between Ash Junction and Farnham Junction. There are intermediate stations at Ash Green and Tongham, and at the latter a portion of the up line has been left as a siding with various connections thereto. These are controlled by two ground frames released by key on the token, and there is also an intermediate key token instrument at Tongham, by means of which a train may be shut into that siding for crossing purposes. This is normal daily practice with one goods train daily, in addition to which the line carries about five passenger trains and one or two goods trains daily in each direction.

'Ash Junction and Farnham Junction now contain old frames of 15 and 16 working levers respectively, with one spare in each case. The alterations to the locking at these boxes and the locking of the ground frames at Tongham are correct. The signals have been abolished at Tongham and a yellow marker light is provided to indicate approach to the station from either direction.

'The line is closed nightly from 9.30 pm to 5.15 am. The company should be asked to submit the usual undertaking as to single line working. The works are complete and in good order and subject to the submission of this undertaking I recommend they be approved.'

This was followed on 24 March 1932 by a simple document headed 'Southern Railway Company' and with the following statement, 'The Southern Railway Company hereby undertake to work the portion of single line railway between Ash Junction and Farnham Junction by the electric key-token system.' The date was as stated and it was signed by W. J. Hatcher of the Secretary's Office. Attached also was the 'Common Seal' of the SR.

Aldershot, looking in the up direction towards Ash Vale, 14 June 1969.
S. W. C. Eyers collection

Thirty to forty years later and Ropley is now unstaffed, the siding has been removed and trains pause briefly to and from Alton. But the topiary is still present … *Rod Hoyle*

Hart – opened 8th October 1849. Name changed Ash to Ash Green in 1876. Ash Green Halt as from 1st December 1926. Closed to passenger traffic 4th July 1937.

Wrecclesham siding (between Farnham and Bentley). Siding in down line. 1 mile 73 chains 13 links from Farnham and 2 miles 0 chains 7 links from Bentley. (1 miles = 80 chains. 1 chain = 100 links. 1 link = just under 8 inches. [7.92 inches].) Siding agreement dated 19th February 1903 between the LSWR and Thomas Patterson of Farnham. Cost of work within Co's boundary £480.

Bentley – Opened July 1854, closed to goods 1st June 1964. Under bridge No 33, from the *Alton Herald*, Friday 15th May 1998. 'Railway disruption. Bentley railway bridge was partially demolished on Wednesday when a lorry collided with it causing rail services between Alton and Farnham to be suspended for an indefinite period. Railtrack engineers were examining the structure in Blacknest Road, Bentley, as The Herald went to press. The parapet on the Bentley station side will be taken down as the structure is unsafe, with the prospect of the track having to be moved to enable rail services to restart. Blacknest Road was closed by Hampshire Police and a permanent diversion has been set up.' A follow-up in the same newspaper the following week included two images, one showing the track deflected some 5ft out of alignment. Services were restored quickly but subject to a 5mph restriction with work to effect a full repair expected to occupy three weeks. In the meanwhile buses were used from Alton whilst some Alton trains started or commenced from Bentley.

From S. W. Smart, 8th May 1934 to Mr Barker 'R' Department. 'Bentley – Bordon branch line. Bentley Junction signal box.' 'Arising out of the proposed extension of electrification to Farnham and the running of a steam shuttle service between Farnham and Alton, it would be possible to make the Bentley – Bordon passenger service a self-contained service running from and to the Down Bay at Bentley. In connection therewith, it has been suggested that the Down bay Line at Bentley be connected with the Bordon branch line independent of the Down Main Line whereby it might be found possible to close Bentley Junction signal box, except where margins are narrow and when required for freight and special troop trains, or for attaching and detaching purposes. Will you please deal with this matter'.

Alton. Opened 28th July 1852. Original station is old building adjoining station on up side. Replaced by station at present position when the line was extended westwards on 2nd October 1865.

Southern Railway Special Instructions to Signalmen at Alton (part). 1933.

'Goods trains must not be allowed to draw forward to the down advanced starting signal to wait 'Line Clear' from Butts Junction or for any other purpose.

The standard branch line 'Train Entering Section' signal will be received and the standard branch line codes must be forwarded for trains to the Meon Valley line.

LSWR Engineer's Office, Waterloo, 12th July 1920. To G F West Esq. Proposed abolition of Ropley, Itchen Abbas and

Shunting bell codes	Number of beats
From east end to signal box	
Open or close up line to No 1 siding points	3 pause 3
Open or close up line to No 2 siding points	1 pause 3 pause 1
Open or close crossover road points	4
Open or close up loop training points	5 pause 1
May train shunt back to platform on up main (wrong) line?	5
Work ground signal for shunting eastwards	1 pause 4
Work ground signal for shunting westwards	4 pause 1
Up train or engine ready to leave	2 pause 3
Up line clear	1 pause 2
Down line clear	2 pause 1
From signal box to east end	
Clear up line	2 pause 2
Clear down line	4 pause 4
From down siding to signal box	
Open or close down line to siding points	2
Down train ready to leave	pause 2
Work ground signal for shunting eastwards	1 pause 4
Work ground signal for shunting westward	4 pause 1
Down line clear	2 pause 1
From signal box to down siding	
Clear down line	4 pause 4
From west end to signal box	
Open or close down line to siding points	2
Open or close crossover road points	4
Open or close up Loop line facing points	1 pause 5
Work ground signal for shunting eastward	1 pause 4
Work ground signal for shunting westward	4 pause 1
Down train ready to leave	3 pause 2

(Remainder of sheet missing.)

Privett as Tablet Sections. 'I return the diagram and plans which accompanied your letter of February 25th last as desired in yours of end instant. The diagrams have been amended in accordance with your request, and when a decision has been come to as to the scheme that is to be adopted I will go into the question of the figures. I am further returning the Privett plan and diagram which has also been amended in accordance with your letter of March 22nd last.'

Further to the above, letter from District Superintendents Office at Waterloo to F Bushrod, dated 24th November 1919. (This time Privett is not mentioned in the subject of the note.) 'With reference to your papers V.32011, from January 1st to October 31st of this year, 135 horse boxes and cattle vans etc. on passenger account were dealt with at Ropley, namely, 69 forwarded and 66 received, and at Itchen Abbas during the same period 32 such vehicles were forwarded and 23 received. I am afraid that in relation to this particular traffic, the contemplated alterations are not calculated to improve the working. In any case it seems to me that the ground signals at each end of the siding points at both stations would be retained in connection with the movements involved in dealing with this class of traffic. I may say that, so far as Ropley is concerned, the horsebox traffic is likely to increase inasmuch as a racing establishment has just been opened near the station, and furthermore, a resumption of hunting (on a large scale) in the neighbourhood is probable. I think that if the schemes are proceeded with the telephone should be removed from the signal boxes to the booking offices, and furthermore some means should be provided of advising the station staff of the approach of trains.'

Alresford as the basic railway in its final years of British Railways operation. The passing loop remains but all sidings, including access to the goods shed, have been removed. The station is also now the last remaining crossing place for services between Winchester and Alton and with all services operated by two or three car DEMU sets. Main line diversions are also semi-regular visitors, especially in the time leading up to the start of the electric services to Bournemouth. Occasionally watercress was still carried, one of the reasons for the retention of the hand barrow – remember them as being once a common sight? Otherwise there is time to stand and chat, to pass the time of day, to put the world to rights, to complain about management … As night falls so the gas light illuminates a deserted platform and booking hall. 'PLEASE SHOW TICKETS' the sign says, but even if well intended, who to? Meanwhile, on another occasion a passenger struggles with luggage … *All Rod Hoyle*

Alresford, opened 2nd October 1865, goods closed 1st June 1964.

Local instructions, dated August 1912.

'After being brought to a stand at the Home signal, a down goods train may be permitted to run into the up Loop line to perform station work, and Station Master must arrange for the train to be hand-signalled forward by a competent man, who must satisfy himself that the facing points are set for the line over which the train is required to run.

'When the station work is completed, the train must be shunted back outside the down Home signal in charge of the hand-signalman, who must satisfy himself that the trailing points are in proper position for the train to pass; the train afterwards being run forward over the down Loop line in the ordinary course.

'When it is necessary for a movement to be made from the west to the east end of the station on the down Loop line, the man in charge of the operation will be held responsible for seeing that the points over which the train or engine will pass are in proper position for the movement to be made.

These signals must be acknowledged by being repeated before they are acted upon.

'If the signalman is unable to comply with any signal be must give the 'Obstruction Danger' signal of 6 continuous beats.

'Should the running line become obstructed in any way by an accident during shunting operations, the shunter must immediately give the 'Obstruction Danger' signal (6 consecutive beats) to the signal box and the signalman must block the line in accordance with Regulation 17 of the Standard Block Regulations for single lines worked on the Electric Train Tablet system, until he has received an assurance from the Station master, or person in charge, that the obstruction has been removed.'

Shunting bell codes	Number of beats
From shunting bell to signal box	
Open or close up loop line to siding points	2
Open or close up loop facing points	4
May train or engine run from west to east end of Station on down loop line?	5
Up loop line clear	1 pause 2
From signal box to shunting bell	
Clear up loop line	2 pause 2

The EPB Story Part 6
The EPB 1951 Stock
BR Standard EPBs Plus Some Extras

David Monk-Steel

With delivery of the Bulleid design of 4EPB under way, consideration was given to the two-car sets necessary to fulfil the requirements of the ten-car scheme. BR had by that time finalised the standard locomotive-hauled carriage designs for both corridor and non-corridor trains, and it was also recognised that there would be insufficient reusable 62ft underframes to supply a complete new fleet of these sets. The choice was therefore made to build the new two-car sets to BR standards, on 63ft 5in underframes with standard BR bogies for the ten-car enhancements. At about the same time the ex-LBSCR A.C. sets that had been converted to D.C. two-car sets for the South London line and West Croydon to Wimbledon line were getting 'tired', so an opportunity here too to deploy new trains was presented.

The construction of these new trains was given to Eastleigh, and because these represented a brand new standard type, Eastleigh remained the main works for all Mark 1 electric stock construction, not only for the Southern Region but for other regions too, throughout the 1950s. Later, the works at York would start electric stock construction in 1958, and by 1964 had taken it over, but that is another story. For the period in question, the required new BR standard underframes were constructed at Ashford instead of Lancing, but were delivered to Eastleigh in a similar fashion.

The first of the new 2EPB sets, No 5701, appeared in January 1954. The next two followed in March and the rest of the first batch, up to No 5711, in June. All were earmarked for the South London Line and Wimbledon to West Croydon service as the stock on these routes was now on its last legs.

The design was superficially similar to the SR 4EPB, but the differences in appearance was noticeable. The stock still retained a flat-fronted appearance at the driving cab end but the proportions of the widths of the three-panel arrangement meant that the centre panel was wider. The arrangement of buffers, coupler, control jumpers, and air brake pipes was at the cab end was the same as the four-car sets. At the inner

The first of new BR Standard 2-coach EPB sets, No 5701 recorded on 6 March 1954. *British Railways*

end, the arrangement of coupler, buffer and jumpers followed the 4EPB pattern, but the end panel was flat. The underframes followed BR standard practice, with the inward facing solebars cantilevered by steel angle from two central trusses, rather than the SR arrangement of trusses beneath the outer solebars. The underframe was entirely of welded construction. Battery boxes and equipment were carried outside the trusses and were thus easier to access. The body profile was generally similar, but the windows instead of being curved to follow the body sheeting were flat glass and the body sheeting pressed to accept this arrangement. The doors were arranged similarly to the four-car sets but omitted the small toplight. Power, control, heating and lighting was the same.

The driver, guard and passengers' accommodation followed closely to the four-car sets as well. The Driving Motor Brake Third (DMBT) had two four-bay saloons instead of a continuous eight-bay one, and the Driving Trailer Third (DTT) had a four-bay saloon and five separate compartments. This arrangement allowed the proportion of smoking to non-smoking seats to be maintained. The driving cab in the Driving Trailer Third was reached via a transverse private vestibule immediately behind it and separated from the passenger accommodation. External doors to this vestibule were inward opening. The bogie underneath the cab in the trailer was a standard non-powered one, but with shoegear attached to the axleboxes. Roof-mounted conduits were a feature of all 1951 type stock.

The 5001, 5101, and 5701 series of units were all regarded as '1951' stock. Construction proceeded until January 1957 with No 5778. The coach numbers were – sets 5701 to 5711 DMBT S65300 to S65310, DTT S77500 to S77510, sets 5712 to 5778 DMBT(DMBS after 1956) S65326 to S65392, DTT(DTS after 1956) S77511 to S77577.

Set 5755 (S65369 & S77554) was reported to swap identities entirely with set 5760 (S65374 & S77559) in June 1956. Set No 5766 was totally destroyed on 4 December 1957 at St Johns when less than 19 months old, and was replaced with a new set 5779, (S65435 & S77578) in June 1958.

Set 5761 (S65375) was fitted with camshaft control gear. Set 5778 was fitted experimentally with Andre Neidhart suspension bogies.

A one-off two car suburban set No 5800 was constructed in January 1960, but was to the later '1957' stock design and more properly belongs with the BR standard four-car suburban stock that will be discussed later.

There were some further two-car suburban sets constructed, however these once again followed the Bulleid design practice of using second-hand 62ft underframes, this time from the 2Nol sets mentioned before. Between October 1959 and December 1959 sets 5651 to 5684 appeared from Eastleigh. The driving motor brake second class coaches (note that third class had become second class in 1956), were identical to the motor coaches in the 5101 series, and were numbered S14557S to S14560S. The Driving Trailer Second

Second class driving trailer of 2 EPB unit No 5747 at Victoria. On this occasion the '2' headcode is likely to refer to a London Bridge/South London line service.

A 2EPB set in later years, reliveried No 5759 at Windsor and Eton Riverside on 10 October 1981. Sets of this type were now designated Class 416/2.
Brian Morrison

saloons numbered S16101S to S16134S consisted of a nine-bay saloon with a driving cab with vestibule between. These sets went on to the Western section immediately they were introduced for use on the Windsor line services. One innovation was the use of self-coloured glass-reinforced plastic in the construction of the outer skin of the doors for these sets (and others produced at this time), which otherwise followed previous Bulleid style exactly.

With the outer suburban business in mind and in anticipation of the first phase of the Kent Coast electrification, a version of the 2EPB stock was introduced in 1957 with first class accommodation and lavatories in the driving trailer. The driving motor brake vehicle was similar to the ones in the 2EPB. 2Hap sets Nos 6001 to 6042 appeared between June 1957 and June 1958. Being similar in formation to the Bulleid 2Hal stock, they progressively replaced them in 1958 on the semi-fast Victoria and Charing Cross to Maidstone and Gillingham services. The first deployment on the Eastern section however was a peculiar feature to placate the well-to-do residents between Sevenoaks and Orpington, who had lost their first class accommodation in ordinary suburban trains in 1941 as a wartime economy measure. It was hoped that, being the first service on which these brand new trains were operating, it

would be received with useful good will. The 8.09am Sevenoaks to Cannon Street was composed of 4EPB and 6Hap shortly after June 1957. The train formed of 2Hap stock returned on the 5.30pm Cannon Street to Sevenoaks, subsequently running empty to Orpington to stable. The displaced 2Hal stock found its way on to the Central division, and eventually became the mainstay of the Victoria to Gatwick service.

The Driving Trailer Composite of the BR 2Hap stock included a second class semi-saloon at the inner end seating fifty, with a door between the foremost seats leading to a single lavatory compartment opening on the right-hand side. Behind the driver's vestibule were a single seven-seat first class compartment and two six-seat non-smoking first class compartments, all linked by a side corridor on the left-hand side in direction of travel, cab leading. An internal swing door separated the seven-seat compartment from the corridor, and sliding doors gave access to the corridor from the other two. All bays and compartments had exterior doors flanked by the usual quarter lights, and an equivalent door was provided opposite each of the two first class smoking compartments. The first class lavatory was entered through a door at the end of the side corridor. There was no communication between first and second class.

An official view of a new 2Hap set No 6005 recorded outside Eastleigh carriage works on 8 November 1957. Nearest the camera is the driving trailer composite with its three first class compartments. *British Railways*

The 2Hap motors were fitted with 'Express 'ratio gears (61/20) to allow for the higher average speeds travelling 'non-stop' for part of the route. This permitted a higher top speed of 90mph. Suburban stock including most EPBs were limited to 75mph, and had gear ratios of 65/16. Regulations later required that at least 50 per cent of trains should be composed of express units where express ratio stock was mixed with suburban.

To finish off the 2Nol conversion programme, further Bulleid design two-car units were constructed on second-hand underframes between February and October 1958. The Driving Motor Brake Second was similar to those in the earlier 4EPBs, but the Driving Trailer Composite vehicle reverted to a layout similar to the 'Tin' 2Hals that had appeared in 1948, placing a single lavatory at the inner end of the carriage, five second class compartments were now behind the driver's vestibule and the three first class compartments between the second class and the lavatory. The corridor went the whole length of the carriage giving access to the sole lavatory. The windows between the doors on the corridor side were combined into a larger pane. The set number series was 5601 to 5636, coach numbers were DMBS S14521S to S14556S and DTC S16001S to S16036S. The body style was pure Bulleid with the EPB flat front and continuous curved body profile.

The last 1951 stock to be built for the Southern Region were twenty-four carriages to the now standard Mark 1 corridor design. These vehicles were gangwayed throughout and formed into four-car motor sets, two sets containing a buffet car of new design, and four entirely containing seating. The motor coaches were loosely based upon the pre-war 4Cor stock with open saloon second class seating in seven bays each seating eight passengers. Access was via transverse vestibules

at either end of the saloon, or via a door in the middle compartment. There were no lavatories provided in the motor coaches. Directly behind the driver was a substantial guards van, which in turn was connected to the front passenger vestibule by a sliding door that the guard or driver could lock as necessary. The driving cab was penetrated by the gangway, and an arrangement of doors alternately closed off the gangway or the driver's cab. This allowed passengers to walk through the intermediate cabs to the adjacent unit without being able to interfere with controls. The route indicator box was attached to the door, which allowed a two window layout in the cab, a considerable improvement over the SR 4Cor 'Nelson' stock. The usual arrangement of high level air brake pipes and control jumper was provided on either side of the gangway connector. Power equipment was similar to the 2Hap. As these were 1951 stock the power, control and lighting conduits were mounted outside on the top of the roof.

At the inner end of each motor coach side buffers were not provided.

The two non-driving carriages were modified locomotive-hauled designs. A Corridor Composite, and a Corridor Second in the all-passenger sets, the Corridor Second being replaced by a buffet car in the buffet sets. The principal differences to a Mark 1 steam carriage was the provision of through electric jumpers, electric heating, electro-pneumatic brakes, fixed head couplers and no side buffers. The steam stock battery boxes and dynamos were also omitted. The outer ends of the motor coached retained buffers and a draw hook carrying the drop-head buck-eye couplers for use in emergencies. Bogies were a modified Mark 1 design, although set 7101 was used for experiments to trial alternatives including the cast Commonwealth type later used on some 1957 stock.

Originally designated 4CorEPB but later changed to 4Cep, Unit 7102 on a test run from Selhurst to Three Bridges, seen passing Redhill. *G. Daniels*

The six sets were originally allocated to the Central Division for the Littlehampton business services.

At first the sets were coded rather clumsily as 4CorEPB and 4BufEPB, but quickly contracted to 4Cep and 4Bep. Set numbers were (4Bep) 7001 and 7002, (4Cep) 7101 to 7104.

The BR type 2EPB stock was extensively used on the Eastern Section for making up ten car sets for the ten-car scheme. Normally they were marshalled at one end of a pair of 4EPB sets. They were attached for the peak services and removed during off peak and at weekends, then stabled to save electricity. A few were used on the Central section for the South London line, the West Croydon to Wimbledon services and as ten-car strengthening to the Tattenham Corner/Caterham service.

The SR style 2EPB sets were, as said above, sent directly to the Western section for the Windsor services.

Initially the 36 SR Type 2Hap and the 1951 type BR style 2Hap were allocated to the Eastern Section in 1958 to displace the 2Hal stock on the Gillingham and Maidstone services which found its way on to the Central and Western section. When the Kent Coast electrification was commissioned (Phase 1 1958 and Phase 2 1962) the 1951 type 2Haps were integrated with the 1957 type 2Haps.

To be continued with The EPB Story: Chapter 7: EPB 1957 and 1960 Stock.

Overleaf: **The original interior of a second class open of a 1958 built Cep unit.** *British Railways*

Terry Cole's Rolling Stock Files No 37
Coach Identification Part 2
Maunsell, Bulleid and BR Mark 1 Coaches

Following on from the previous Rolling Stock File, we look this time at later coaching stock. My comments are again generalisations but will I hope prove useful to the layman. In all previous Files I have refrained from including any preserved railway vehicles but make an exception this time, featuring pictures of coaches on the Bluebell Railway.

This is the compartment side of a Maunsell 'Restriction 4' coach in Departmental service condition with some non-original additions. It clearly illustrates the body outline with relatively straight sides then curving to the underframe at the bottom. The Restriction '1' and '0' variants, which I covered extensively in previous Files, had flat sides. With the exception of two early batches of Bulleid compartment stock (which I hope to cover in a future issue), all Bulleid and BR Mark 1 corridor stock had large 'picture' windows and no doors giving direct platform access from the compartments.

This is No 4279, an example of an early Bulleid corridor coach. It is a semi-open brake third built by the Birmingham Carriage and Wagon Company with narrow window ventilators characteristic of early Bulleid designs. The continuous curved side profile of the coach is echoed by the curves in the windows and doors. The adjacent coach, also a Bulleid vehicle, has the later much deeper window ventilators. This later style was much more numerous.

Here we have a pair of BR Mark 1s on a train at Horsted Keynes. The coach sides are very similar to Bulleid coaches, especially the later ones, with the same curved profile, picture windows and large window ventilators. There is, however, a cast iron method of identifying Mark 1s – look at the underframe. Maunsell or Bulleid vehicles have the truss rods (which support the underframe and stop it bending) at the outside edges of the underframe. Mark 1s, on the other hand, have them set about a third of the way in from each side so making them effectively invisible in most photographs. (These coaches also have Commonwealth bogies; an additional identification point.) So if you can't see the truss rods on a coach then it's a Mark 1!

The Isle of Wight O2s in the 1930s

A few years ago soon after SW had started, our good friend Dave Hammersley (he of Roxey Mouldings) loaned us an album of snapshot type prints, mainly Southern, taken in the 1930s. Unfortunately some were exactly as described, snapshots, taken to record a now forgotten enthusiasts meanderings around the railway but also sadly unsuitable for reproduction. Fortunately included in the album were a number from the Isle of Wight, principally static views of the O2s but with a smattering of E1s as well. Regretfully no locations were given whilst as the individual engines are also readily identified there is little point in captions simply pointing out the obvious. 'Pride in the job' might be said to be a common theme, the engines clean and evidently well cared for whilst on the occasions when a crew is also visible there is a proudness displayed there too. Purely for a bit of fun, readers might like to try and work out the locations where they were taken for themselves. No prizes, and whilst one or two are obvious, Bembridge with No 22 for example, we are not sure we could be totally accurate with all of the others. So you Isle of Wight experts can you help? We will publish the results in a future issue.

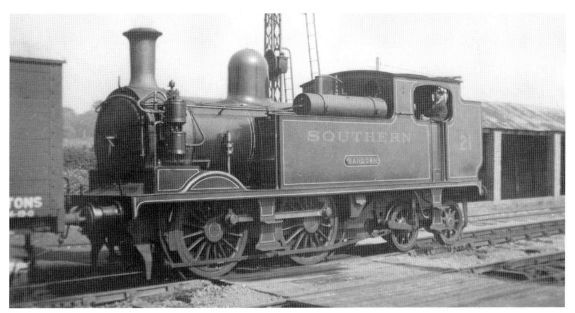

The Last Word
More on No. 35004

No 21C2 at Salisbury 20-9-47 clearly with a leak/split in the tank; likewise patch between second and third axle T3117 attached to 35003, which was one of five rebodied (into 5,250gal) along with T3111/35001, T3112/35002, T3115, T3117/35003 & T3118/35008.

And then this arrived from Mark Arscott – he who produces some very useful wheels for the 4mm modeller and some useful tools suitable for all gauges. ('Mar-Kits') Mark is an avid Bulleid man and reported as follows:

'Are you sitting comfortably?' 'Yes …?' 'Ref *SW* No 35 … you asked about the tender to 35004 when it was scrapped at Eastleigh mpd.

'35004 arrived with T3113 (original 5000gal) which it had acquired in 1/1944. Its original tender T3114 had gone to 21C7 in 5/44, probably because T3117 (21C7) had developed splits in the tank, which was made from 3/16in Plate and then later changed to ¼in …

'The 1st and 3rd Series Tender Tank drawings are shown to be made from 3/16in, but the 2nd Series states ¼in.

'T3115 originally attached to 21C5 converted into Mechanical Berkley Stoker 3/48 with a temporary swap to No 35002 in 3/52 and returned also in 3/52 and rebodied 5/59 when No 35005 was rebuilt.

'By 1/44 T3113, which … But I digress … in early 1944 Nos 35003, 35004 & 35007 were all in Eastleigh Works, and T3113 had additional Wash Plates fitted.

Following on from the recent piece on the demise of No 35004, I have been genuinely touched by the number of readers who have sent in kind comments about the article, none more so that Peter Hopkins who added, ' … you are wrong to say nothing from No 35004 survived.' Thank you Peter, assuming also the name and number plates are now in various collections, all we need to find is a frame, some wheels, cylinders, boiler, clack valves, rods, smokebox, buffers …

T3114 attached to No 35003 at Eastleigh on 20 May 1958.

'It left the works attached to No 35004, was modified/cut-down in 6/58 when the loco was rebuilt.

'It retained T3113 until the high speed slip on 28 October 1965, between Basingstoke and Hook whilst working the 07.24 Bournemouth–Waterloo.

'The loco was removed to Eastleigh, with severely bent rods on both sides and probably also damaged inside motion.

'Deemed uneconomically repairable, officially withdrawn 10/65, was 'written-off' for scrap, sold to Cohens but presumably 'unmovable'.

'However, T3113 must have been deemed serviceable as it was then allocated to 35029 and the whole ensemble ended at the NRM York, sectionalised.

'Meanwhile, 35029 had been attached to 6,000gal 'T3347', following a 'Light Intermediate' overhaul 7/52, was given T3129, a 5,100gal, presumably the T3347/6,000gal deemed unnecessary for work on the Eastern Section, and then partnered with 35022.

'Upon withdrawal in 5/66, No 35022 was sold to Woodham's, Barry, whilst the tender was sold on to Britton Ferry Steel Works, where the frames and wheels were used as ingot carriers.

'Presumably T3121 attached to 35011 was not in the best of health and so was swapped with the tenderless 35004 (presumably being sold to the scrap merchant as 'Locomotive AND Tender').

'Likewise 35011 and T3129 found their way to Woodham's, albeit 35011 with THREE plain driving axles (no crank axle for the middle cylinder!) and T3129 joined T3347 at Briton Ferry Steel Works, along with thirteen Light Pacific tender chassis.'

So now we know!

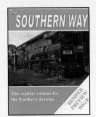
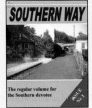
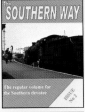

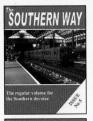
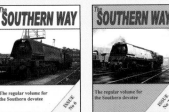

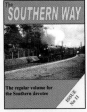
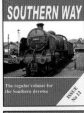
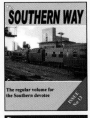
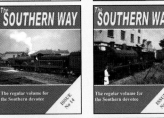

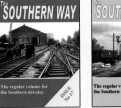

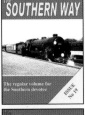

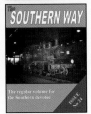
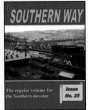
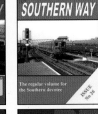

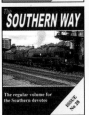
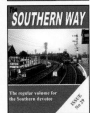
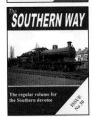
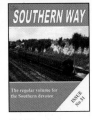
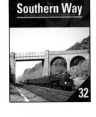
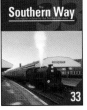
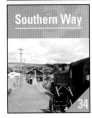
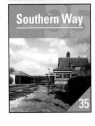
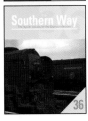
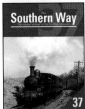